Mountain Moving Mama

A True Story of Life, Death, & the Power of Prayer

By Betty Green
As told to Leslie Graham

Mountain Moving Mama: A True Story of Life, Death, & the Power of Prayer

Published by Leslie Graham LLC

All Scripture quotations, unless otherwise indicated, are taken from the King James Version of the Bible (KJV).

Printed in the United States of America.

ISBN-13: 978-1-7343810-0-9

Disclaimer: Some names or identities have been changed to protect individual privacy.

Dedication

This book is dedicated to both of my mama's and to all the mama's who want the very best for their children – to know and to love Jesus.

This preface, written by Dr. Ja-Shil Choi, accompanied Betty's book, From Vice to Victory, when she originally published her story.

It is my prayer that you read this book, as I have learned to love Betty Green as a daughter. Betty has traveled for three years all over the world with me. We have carried the message of fasting and prayer. God has let Betty catch my vision, together we will start this fasting and prayer movement all over the world. I have seen Betty tell her testimony many times, and many people were saved, lives were touched. I believe you will be, as you read how God changed Betty's life. Today she is a great women of God. God has given Betty the gift of healing. Not only should you read this book, but God has blessed Betty to write twelve books on prayer, fasting, healing, self, and pride. I believe you will be very blessed through this book of Betty Green's life story. Fast! Fast! Pray! Pray!

Jashil Choi

목사려 자실
Choi ga shil

Table of Contents

Foreword

———————————

I wish to congratulate apostle Betty Green, known as "Mama Betty" for such a timely and very inspirational book.

Her inspiring story, anointed ministry and dynamic message has brought transformation, revelation and wisdom to generations of people worldwide.

In 1985, while praying for a group of 12 inner city pastors in Los Angeles, California, she was led of the Holy Spirit of God to prophesy to me 3 individual times during the service. Each time, telling me in more detail that, "God was going to mightily use me in television around the globe."

On March 2nd, 2015, the Lord supernaturally commissioned me to launch the Holy Spirit Broadcasting TV Network and within 4 years, we were being viewed in 186 countries by millions of people. Additionally, I have had the awesome privilege of being elevated to "Apostle" of our global HSBN movement, as she and others laid their mantles upon me.

As an authentic "seer" and apostle, she preaches the Word of God and only says what the Holy Spirit instructs her to say. I have personally stood next to her at the front of prayer lines and witnessed God reveal problems or conditions and saw God's miraculous presence at work, healing many through her laying on of hands.

She's been mightily used of the Lord to prophesy to many, and the results have been amazing. God always watches over his word to perform it.

She has a very lengthy history of being used as a servant of God globally, and I totally recommend her teaching and ministry to all to enjoy and be blessed by.

I love "Mama Betty" and believe in the spirit of our living Christ within her.

Dr. Andrew Bills
Apostle & founder of the Holy Spirit Broadcasting TV Network

1

In the Beginning

Mama was a very smart woman. I learned a lot of things by watching my mama.

I learned a thing or two from watching other family members, too.

Mama's sister, my Aunt Susie Mae, married their cousin, Jack, and it was quite the scandal. The family disowned her for marrying him. There was simply no peace there. Jack's sister was the wife of my daddy's brother, so Uncle Jack was still allowed to visit at our place.

Uncle Jack liked to drink, but he couldn't handle liquor at all. He was mean when he was drunk, and he'd beat Susie Mae. She often begged me not to tell him things because he'd beat her. She wasn't supposed to go see her parents. But, when her brother's body was shipped back to the states from the war, she had to go say good-bye.

All the way home, Susie Mae cried. "Betty, please don't tell Jack."

"I ain't gonna talk to him," I whispered.

"If you do, he'll beat me from here 'til tomorrow," she whispered back.

"I'm afraid he'll beat me too," I replied. I was afraid of him when he was drinking.

Jack's drinking was bound to get him into trouble sooner or later. Thankfully, I wasn't there to witness it when that fateful day happened. My cousins later shared this story with me.

You see, Mama's brothers had a still for making moonshine. When Jack got mad one day, and decided to tell on them, the cops came over and blew it up.

Those brothers were sure Jack had something to do with it, so they went across the hill and put kerosene in Jack's still. When he found out, he was MAD. The kerosene ruined the whole thing and he couldn't use it no more.

"Susie Mae, come on. We gonna go find out what's going on," Jack commanded.

The two of them walked up the hill to our house carrying guns. They thought for sure they would get Mama to tell them what really happened, because they knew that Mama wouldn't lie. She was a Christian. They actually thought she was going to tell on her brothers. Imagine that.

Daddy was taking a nap in his bedroom when they pulled up. From what I'm told, Daddy didn't wear shorts. And, he'd never wear his work clothes in bed.

Susie Mae came running into the room, "Tom!", she screamed.

Startled, Daddy throwed the sheet back and jumped out of bed. "Huh? What's going on?" He looked to see Susie Mae standing there with a gun pointed right at him.

Jack had sent Susie Mae in to shoot my daddy.

Susie Mae, too afraid to shoot, started yelling at him. "Tom, don't!" She knew that him standing there naked before her would give her an excuse that would keep Jack from killing her, too. Embarrassed, she ran out the house.

Daddy put on his pants and went outside to see what was going on.

"Come here you (so and so)," Uncle Jack yelled at Daddy.

"Now, Jack. You're drunk. Get your tail on down the road before something goes wrong. You ain't got no business up here hollerin' and messin' around."

"Aw, hell, Tom, I'm gonna kill you and Rene," Jack snarled.

Mama went to talk to Jack out by the roadside. She wanted to send him on his way before things got out of hand. As they stood there talking, Jack slapped Mama.

Seeing this, Daddy went and grabbed his shotgun. "Now, Jack. Git your butt on down the road. There ain't gonna be no sh@! goin' on around here."

"Hell no! I ain't goin' no darn wheres. I'm gonna kill you and Rene. Then, I'm gonna run your kids off like these chickens – out over the hills. And I'll kill a few of them along the way too!"

THAT was the wrong thing to say to my daddy. Those were fightin' chickens – worth $500 apiece, and the way Daddy made a livin'. He made a lot of money fightin' them birds. He was probably madder about the threat to his chickens than he was his kids.

Jack raised his gun.

"Drop it!" Daddy said, his shotgun pointing directly at Jack.

Jack jumped down into the creek for cover so that he could shoot Daddy. As he jumped, he turned, and Daddy's gun went off catching Jack in the back of the shoulder.

Susie Mae jumped down after him, dropping her gun in the process.

"Jack!" Susie Mae cried out. Jack moaned in pain.

"Now, Susie Mae," Daddy called to her. "You throw the guns up and I'll take him to the hospital. But I ain't coming down there 'til you throw the guns up."

Susie Mae threw Jack's gun up onto the bridge.

"You've got one too. Now, you throw it up." Jack continued to groan. "Don't you do it, Susie Mae," Jack threatened.

"I can't find it!" Susie Mae cried. She frantically looked and hunted all over trying to find the gun she had in her hand moments earlier. Finally, her gun appeared on the bridge as well.

Daddy jumped down into the creek. "Jack, why'd you have to go and do this?" He lifted Uncle Jack up onto the bridge, climbed up himself, and then put Jack in the back of his pick-up to drive him to the hospital. Susie Mae jumped in back, too, cradling Jack in her arms.

Halfway there, Jack says, "Susie Mae . . . raise me up. Let me see the son of a b.... who killed me."

Then, he died in her arms.

Just a night or two before, the preacher had called Uncle Jack out in church.

"We can't count on anything but the Lord. Would you like to come to Jesus tonight?" the preacher asked.

"Hell no!" Jack cussed at him.

"Jack," the preacher said, "you are going to bust hell wide open."

Most people would be too ashamed to share this story. This is my family. I love them deeply, but it's stories like these that I fear will make us sound so dumb, especially by today's standards. This may have been normal living in the mountains of North Carolina during the 1940's and '50's, but I'm so far from that now, sometimes it seems like a separate life. I guess in many ways it is exactly that.

I considered keeping this kind of thing out of this book, but God knows my real story. He loves me in spite of it.

Nowadays, people know me as a powerful ambassador of Jesus. When I preach, almost everybody in the church gets healed or demons are cast out. There have been times where every person in the place gets slain in the Spirit. I'm not sure why God decided to use me as He has. I am only grateful that He has done so.

I remember the time when I was preaching in Houston, TX. I was handed the mic when a 17-year-old boy who was deaf and dumb approached the platform, at one of my crusades. I cast that deaf and dumb spirit out of him, and he heard for the very first time in his life! 15,000 people come up out of their seats, screaming and hollering, praising God.

Or, there was the time when I prayed for Pastor Kim's wife. Her daughter was in the hospital recovering from an aneurysm. When I come off the pulpit, during a service at Prayer Mountain, I went over to pray with her, as two mothers praying together for her daughter. As I moved toward her, I looked, and I "seen" (I'm a seer, so I see in the Spirit). I saw that her whole breast was black. I had a vision of the inside of her breast.

I said, "I can't pray for your daughter. You've got breast cancer in the fourth stages and I've got to pray for you right now!"

When I pray for cancer, I see a fire come and blaze right into it. It burned it right out of her.

That same night, another girl came up and asked for prayer. She wanted to have a baby. She had been praying and asking God seven years to bless her with a child. I told her God was going to give her a baby and what that baby was going to be.

The next time I went there to preach at Prayer Mountain in Romoland, California, Pastor Kim was taking a long time to introduce me. I wondered why. He was speaking in Korean, so I didn't know what he was saying.

I leaned over and whispered to the girl next to me, "What is he talking about? It's taking a long time,".

She answered, "Oh, he is telling about how nobody knew that his wife had cancer but when you prayed you told her she had cancer of the breast."

They'd told no one, because her daughter was in the hospital fighting for her life. She wanted to take no chance that her daughter would find out. God healed her of that breast cancer. She is still living to this very day.

And that girl? She had that baby, just as I'd told her she would.

If I can be honest with you for just a moment, I tell you I can understand exactly how David felt when he confronted that giant. If I were faced with someone confronting my beliefs with the threat of imminent death, I would stand there firmly saying, "Who do you think you are? I want to tell you about my God!!"

I believe that I could ask God to rain fire down from heaven. And I believe that fire would be right on their heels and they would be running as fast as they could to get away from me. All along, that fire would be just trying to consume them. They would receive Jesus, or they would die! I believe God is that big. I believe God is AWESOME.

This is the kind of Spirit filled person I am.

I know when some read this, they'll be looking for that preacher they've seen in church or on TV. People are used to experiencing the kind of anointing I have. But way before I was that person, I was someone far different.

It is important that I share my "before" so that you can fully appreciate my "after".

So many people feel as though they are nobody. They don't feel good about themselves. They think they can never achieve the life that they dream about. I just want you to see what God can really do in your life. It doesn't matter how bad you get! When you repent, God still forgives you.

When you read the pages of my life story, I want you to look at how bad I really was. Jesus, quite literally, saved me from the ravages of hell. And the fact that God could forgive me and use me so mightily for His purposes, with such a strong anointing, is the best evidence I have for the message of eternal salvation. He turned my life around SO much!! That is what I want you to see... THAT is the real miracle. And He'll do the same for you.

2

A Girl in the Mountains

One of my earliest memories was of my cousin, Mattie. I loved her so much.

"Maybe, I'll get some new clothes today, Mama," I said with a smile.

Mama did not return the smile. "Get dressed, Betty," she replied in her deep southern accent. "It's time for us to go."

"Yes, ma'am."

The wood stove nearby tried its best to keep us warm, but the cool winter air continued to creep in.

Before long, we were headed to my aunt and uncle's house. It was not too far away.

I was so excited. I was going to see Mattie today! Mattie was my favorite cousin. She was such a pretty little thing. Her curly blonde hair was something to be admired. And those beautiful blue eyes of hers, they were a lot like me and my mama's. She definitely took after Mama's side of the family.

Every summer and every winter, I would get me some new hand me down clothes from Mattie. She was small for a seven-year-old, but since she was a year older than me that worked out fine. I was just the right size to get her clothes as she grew out of them. All of my shoes, clothes—everything I ever got came from Mattie.

Through the trees, barren from winter's kiss, I could see her house in the distance. Mama, Daddy, my siblings and I made our way up the dirt road that led to the tiny, wooden, four-square house nestled in the woods. As we passed the nearby creek, I remembered warmer days when Mary and Marshall, Mattie's brother and sister, and I would go swimming with her.

Approaching the door to the house, I could hear the gentle rumble of words passed between those who were inside. All of my aunts and uncles, cousins and kin were there—dozens and dozens of us. My grandmother had eighteen children and they all had lots of children of their own. And, they were all there.

Inside, the heat of all those bodies kept us extra warm against the cold winter air, which was nice since indoor heating was a luxury not yet invented. Heck, we didn't even have electric or indoor plumbing in our homes. The money to pay for a pole to be installed so as we could have the power hooked up was not something our families could afford.

As we entered the front door, I could see Mattie right there in the living room. She was sleeping in the prettiest little white box I had ever seen.

I ran to Mattie's side, grabbed her hand and tugged on her arm. "Mattie. Mattie wake up. Let's go play!" I said excitedly.

But Mattie didn't move.

"Come on, Betty," Mama said, grabbing my hand.
"Leave Mattie be. Let's go get you something to eat."

I turned to look back at Mattie as we walked away. "Why won't she wake up?" I wondered.

Family members had come that day with enough food to share with one and all. It was like an indoor family picnic, but not nearly as fun. The day passed and Mattie never did wake up to play with me. Then, the time came.

Slowly, we all walked to the family burial ground in back of Granny and Granddaddy's house down the road. I watched as Mattie's parents, my aunt and uncle, solemnly made their way to a hole in the ground. With them, was that pretty little white box, and Mattie sleeping peacefully inside. I watched as they lowered the box into the hole in the ground, covering it over with dirt.

I'd had two other cousins, about the same age as me, just like Mattie. They went to sleep and didn't wake up either. I went to every funeral. I looked on as each of them was lowered into a hole in the ground.

"I must be next," I thought to myself.

In my naïve child's mind, I thought for sure that one day they were going to do that to me. To this day, I refuse to let anybody put me in the ground. I done bought me a box (crypt) above ground. Traumatic things like this affect children their whole life.

Once Mattie went to sleep that day, the clothes stopped coming. I had no new clothes that year. All winter long I had no shoes. I wore the same old pair of galoshes, which had a hole in one end and my feet were always freezing cold. Eventually my teacher asked another little girl at school if she could spare a pair of her shoes for me. I was so proud of those new shoes!

I was the sixth child born to a poor family in the mountains of North Carolina during the heart of the Great Depression. Our home wasn't much, but it was enough. We had a living room with a big wood stove at one end. Our kitchen was long with room for a table big enough to seat sixteen. The doctor Mama had worked for gave her a nice set of furniture with the table and a china cabinet, though we never had any china to put inside.

I had lots of brothers and sisters. I didn't know it then, but eventually there would be thirteen of us in all. Unfortunately, I never met my older brother Herby Joe.

He died at the age of three from pneumonia, before I was ever born.

Upstairs, there were two tiny bedrooms. We had no closets nor dressers. Our clothes were stored in boxes under the stairs.

The chimney from that wood stove came up through the middle of the house, so it was always nice and warm upstairs. The heat coming off of it kept us cozy.

All of us girls slept together in one bedroom with the younger brothers. We had two beds in that room. The girls in one bed, the boys in the other.

Mama had made us a straw tick for each of those beds, in place of a mattress. Now, the nice thing about a straw tick is that if one of us wet the bed, it would go right down into the straw and so you wouldn't have to lay in a wet spot all night. You could easily take it outside, air it out during the day, and you'd never notice the difference.

We had hundreds of chickens, so we saved feathers up and Mama would make us this big ol' thing that she stuffed full of them. We didn't have a lot of quilts and blankets and stuff like that. Instead, this feather bed is what we used as our cover. When you'd get down there and snuggle under that feather bed, it would keep the heat in your body. So, that's how we slept. It was awesome!

The older boys slept in the second bedroom. Mama and Daddy slept in their big bedroom downstairs. It was a pretty cramped and cozy set up for fourteen people to live in.

A few months passed after Mattie's funeral and I started school. The dirt roads twisting through the mountains were a challenge for those old school buses. One day, as my bus came through the winding road headed to my house, a car approached us, head on.

"Hold on!" the driver shouted as the bus swerved.

He'd tried to clear the way for the car, but the heavy school bus was too much for the embankment which quickly gave way and caved in.

Children screamed as over and over, the full bus toppled and turned on itself. Bodies were bouncing off of the seats and off of each other as there were no seatbelts to hold us in place.

The bus turned over three times before finally landing at the end of the steep embankment. I nearly got my own little white box that day.

In no time at all, word got out and everyone's parents were rushing to the scene of the accident. I was unconscious when my daddy pulled me out from underneath my seat. I don't know how I got there. Next thing I know, Daddy had put us all in the back of his truck and took us to the hospital. I had three cracked vertebrae from that accident. Thankfully, it was not my time to die.

I was terrified of dying.

Nobody explained to me anything about death. At night, our home would get real dark in those wooded mountains. We had nothing but a kerosene lamp to make our way through the darkness. I was so afraid that if I would close my eyes that I would not wake up again. That was the way it happened with my little cousins. Every night, I would cry and cry, until I fell asleep.

"Bet, go to sleep," Mama yelled. She didn't come up the stairs to comfort me. In those days, affection was not shown. That was a private thing.

"Mama, I can't shut my eyes. If I do, I might die."

"You're not gonna die. I said go to sleep!"

But I didn't want to close my eyes. If I did, I knew for sure I'd be visited once again by that terrible dream. Almost every night I'd dream that I had to jump across a well of snakes. And every night I'd fall into that well. Those snakes would crawl all over me, flipping and flopping around. I'd wake up screaming and screaming until Mama would call up the stairs.

I was so sure I was going to die in my sleep. I didn't understand about death. Nobody explained it to me, ever. It's awful to learn the hard way. There were so many things I would learn the hard way.

3

Moonshine Wars

One day, Mama and me were at my granddaddy's house when several politicians stopped in. A bunch of them came together for lunch and some white lightning (moonshine). In those days, it wasn't legal, but all the men liked drinking it. Of course, Granddaddy told 'em he knew someone who had some good white lightning. They didn't know it was his sons who were making it.

My granddaddy had a lot of influence in the region. He owned 500 acres of land, as did his brothers and sisters too. Plus, he had 18 children who also owned land. He was well known and had a lot of power. Congressmen and senators would personally visit Granddaddy to get his endorsement. In fact, so well-known and respected was he that he could put 'em in and take 'em out of office.

I was sitting near Mama while she washed the dishes. She had just cleared the plates from the table after the gentlemen's lunch. One of the congressmen had followed her into the kitchen.

"Can I get you a cup of coffee?" she asked. Mama always did have good manners.

"I'd like that," he smiled.

Mama got the congressman a cup of coffee and then continued washing dishes as they talked with one another.

"Ya know...sure would be good to have a black top. These dirt roads up in the mountains can be something dangerous. Why I almost lost my children in a bus accident a few months ago because of those roads."

"Really?"

"Yes sir. Ya know, a car come at their school bus, head on. And when the bus driver swerved to avoid the car, the bus rolled over and over down a steep embankment because the dirt gave way."

By the time Mama was done with him, he had agreed to put a new two-lane highway through there. Once he was elected, he made good on that promise. Not only that, he got us electricity too.

I learned a lot of things by watching my mama.

I was at Granddaddy's when I heard the explosion from Jack's moonshine still being blown to pieces. By the time I'd made my way home, Daddy was already back from dropping Jack off at the hospital.

I saw the police cars sitting in the driveway as I approached the house. I had no idea what was going on, but something told me it wasn't good.

As I entered the house, Mama was sitting at the table crying hysterically. Daddy, covered in blood, was removing his shirt. The Sherriff was standing there waiting for him.

"Put a clean shirt on before we go, Tom," the Sheriff said.

They didn't handcuff Daddy. They knew my daddy and they knew he wasn't a mean man. He wouldn't blow someone away for no reason.

About that time, Aunt Kae arrived and took Mama and us children home with her. When we got to my aunt's house, one of my cousins told me what happened.

It was a sad time for all of us. I hurt so deeply when Uncle Jack died. During the weeks and months before all this happened, I had spent quite a lot of time with my aunt and uncle. I used to babysit their little boy. He was a sweet little boy.

Other times, I'd just go to their house and stay a few nights while I helped around the house. I loved staying at their house so much!

When he wasn't drinking, Uncle Jack was a kind, loving man. And whenever the pastor would ask him to come to church, he'd go.

As a grown woman looking back, I wish that the pastor had not been so harsh on Uncle Jack. You've got to love people. I think that if he could have shown him more love Uncle Jack might have turned it around.

We've got to be so careful with the things we say to people. We can cause someone to not make it to heaven because of our words, and then their blood would be on our hands.

Ultimately, Daddy was sentenced to 3 to 7 years in the state penitentiary. I was now 10 years old and my daddy was in prison.

It was like a war while Daddy was gone, sort of like the Hatfield's and the McCoy's. Jack's dad and brothers put a sign up on their land that read, "If any Suddreths come across this hill, we'll blow 'em away". We had to put up with quite a lot from them while Daddy was gone.

Everybody in town knew that my daddy had killed a man, so it hurt us in school, too.

"Murderers!" Kids, at school, would call us that and everything else.

Even the teacher made fun of me. One day, she was fussing at me about studying or something.

"My daddy, he never went to school and he makes more money than most men." I answered, sarcastically.

16

"Yeah, he's real smart," she replied. "He just killed a man and he's in prison."

We didn't understand why they were so mean to us.

By December of my sixth-grade year, I was taken out of school. That is all the schooling I ever got. My sister had gotten married and my mother needed to work, so I had to stay home to take care of the little ones. She was working for Dr. McNeary, helping deliver babies. Mama would also take care of the office and sterilize all of the doc's tools.

My mother was such a godly woman. She was the oldest girl in her family and her sisters really loved her and honored her. They felt so bad for us, so they would help when they could. Debra was one of Mama's sisters.

While Daddy was away, Aunt Debra would give us a gallon of buttermilk every day. And every single day, I would walk miles to get that gallon of buttermilk.

Times was tough for us while Daddy was gone. For weeks and weeks, it seemed that all we ate was cornbread and that slimy, canned spinach that the welfare had brought us. I hated that spinach, but we had no choice—eat it or go hungry.

I wanted so badly for Mama to love me and I looked for ways to impress her. I would work hard to clean the house up and make it pretty, wanting so badly for her to say just one sweet thing or tell me what a good job I'd done. I never got nothin'! I don't know why people didn't encourage little ones back then, but I'm glad to see that happens more nowadays.

Daddy was released for good behavior after only eighteen months in prison. If only his behavior at home would be good.

He owned his own landscaping business. All the rich people in town used it. My brothers worked for him, though sometimes Daddy would hire a cousin of mine, too. He would dress up and get all the jobs, and they would do all the work.

I believe if Mama hadn't gone to work, Daddy would've come through for us. He always took good care of us, even when we still lived at Granddaddy's house. But, now that Mama was working, Daddy began to lose interest.

I think sometimes when us women start working, it makes it more difficult for our men to show us how terrific they are as providers. I think it may somehow injure their manhood.

I wanted Mama's attention more than anything and I thought that she would love me more if I would tell on Daddy. After all, when my sisters would tell on me, she seemed to love them more.

So, when I found that cigarette butt in Daddy's truck, I just knew I had to tell her.

You see, Daddy wasn't a Christian. When Mama got saved, Daddy started running around. I was about six or seven years old then. We had just moved from my mother's big family home to our new house, close to Mama's family. After that, Daddy was gone most of the time and it all went downhill from there.

My daddy was the best-looking man that ever walked the face of this earth. Every woman in town was after him. I thought it was awful and I was not going to let him get away with it.

I marched proudly into the house, ready to deliver my news. Mama and Daddy were sittin' at the kitchen table laughin' and havin' the best time drinkin' coffee.

I lifted the lipstick covered cigarette butt in the air and declared, "Look here, Mama. Daddy has been out with a whore again."

Daddy stormed out of the room.

18

Mama was so mad at me. "Bet, why do you want to hurt me? You've been a curse from day one," she shouted as tears streamed down her face. "While I was having you, I looked out the window from the hospital and seen your daddy with another woman. And I thought, if it wasn't for you, he wouldn't be out there, and I wouldn't be in here."

She went on, "I knew you had a spirit. Your grandma thinks so too."

Did I feel unloved? Yes. Rejected? For sure. But I had no demons. I was haunted only by the spirit of rejection.

Maybe that was why I was so shy. Of course, I was brave with my family, but any time strangers would come around I would do my best to hide. If someone came to our house, I would hide behind the door. That's just how shy and timid I was. I'm sure that the bullying at school, and the rejection I felt at home, had something to do with it.

I ran from the house. Tears poured out my eyes.

"Nobody loves me," I cried to myself. I was the black sheep of the family. My brothers and sisters would lie and get me beat all the time for things I didn't do. Mama didn't want me. Daddy cared more about his chickens than me. I just wanted someone to love me.

I made up my mind. I didn't feel like something special, but I said, "I'm going to be something one day. I'll prove to everybody that I am special!"

4

Child Bride

Spring was so beautiful in those Carolina mountains and the smell of magnolia reached into every corner of our home. It didn't take away the drudgery of working on the farm, but it sure did make it look prettier. The hills were lined with all types and colors of flowers.

I was up by 5 am every mornin'. Then, I'd get the younger ones up and off to school. Mama would go to work and Daddy, well... Daddy often slept in until 10 or so. Then he'd get up and leave, too. I spent all day, every day, feeling alone—just me, my little brothers and sisters, and the chickens. There was no one my age to talk to.

After washing the clothes on the scrub board, I hung them on the line to dry in the crisp spring air.

"I guess I should start planting some pepper plants," I said to myself.

I was covered in mud by the time the preacher dropped by. He was kin with my mama, so he often came by to check in on me.

"Betty, come over here and meet my friend, Larry," said the preacher. "He works with me at the shop." Back then, preachers had to hold regular jobs so they could make a livin'. They usually didn't make enough to survive as a preacher otherwise.

I walked over to greet my visitors. It was nice to have someone to talk to, even if only for a little while.

I was so embarrassed. I chastised myself silently. "Oh, my hair is a mess and I am so dirty. You knew the preacher was gonna come by today. Why didn't you get cleaned up?"

There was something about this man, Larry, but I didn't know anything about relationships with men back then. He was easily several years my senior—a grown man for sure. I was only fourteen years old.

"Howdy, ma'am," Larry nodded towards me.

"Hello, sir. Nice to meet you," I nervously replied as I glanced to the ground.

I could tell he liked me. His eyes locked on my chest. He watched my every move so intently. I didn't know how to act. The only men I'd ever been around were my kin and, of course, the schoolboys, but that had been years ago.

Larry came to church with the pastor and the pastor's son and daughter, to sing for us and quickly became a part of our church family. It was easy for him to fit in. He was friendly and outgoing. As a guitar player and a singer, I suppose that personality of his came in handy.

Finally, one day, he came to our house. I answered the door.

"Is your mama home?" he asked.

"Mama, Larry's here to see you," I called to her.

Mama came to the door.

"What's goin' on here?" Mama asked. I could tell by the expression on her face that she was very suspicious of this visit.

"Ma'am, I'd like to ask permission to take Betty to church with me."

Mama, with her hand on one hip, tilted her head and thought for a moment. "Ok then, but Nona has to go with her."

Larry smiled. "Thank you, ma'am," he said excitedly.

I'd never been around a man who was interested in me the way Larry was. The way he looked at me... it made me real nervous. So, I sat my little sister, Nona, between us that night.

Over time, Larry came to our house more and more until it seemed he was over every evenin'. We sat on the back of his car talkin' and talkin'. Physically, I was developing into a woman. Emotionally, I was still very much a child.

Even with all this time spent together, I was never fully comfortable with him. I could tell he was crazy about me, but I didn't like him. I don't know why Mama and Daddy let him come over so often, except that I was the right age for a mountain girl to be married off. Mama and Daddy probably considered him a good prospect. He always wore a hat and a suit. Being ten years older than me and having steady employment was certainly a good sign to them. He was the son of a Baptist preacher, what more could a parent want? To me, he was an old man.

When I turned fifteen, Larry and I started singin' in church together. I loved goin' to church. It was the only place I was ever able to go except for home and visitin' relatives.

And I really loved singin'. Church songs were great, but country music, man, I loved that even better. We became very popular in the area and other churches began to ask us to visit so as we could come and sing and play for them.

The four of us, pastor's son and daughter, Larry, and me travelled and played music together a lot. Pastor picked the music and we played. Larry sang the lead.

During this time, I wanted the Holy Spirit so bad. One night, I went to sit down at the altar and fell out in the Spirit. I saw Jesus standing over me with His hands stretched out to me. I started speaking in tongues to Him; I was so happy. It gave me such joy!

Another night, I went to church with my friend Sally. Afterwards, we still wanted to spend time together.

"Come on over my house, Betty. Please..." she pleaded.

I knew I was supposed to get home, but I wanted to spend time with my friend so badly. I said, "Ok".

It didn't take long before night fell, and Sally's parents urged me to sleep over. Larry, having already been to my house, had come to visit too. Sally's parents really liked him. He was almost their age. They knew he was crazy about me and wanted to help the courtship along, so they invited me to stay.

I knew I was supposed to be home on Sunday nights, because I had to take care of the kids on Monday morning. I loved Sally's house and if I could, I'd stayed there forever, but I just knew if I stayed that Daddy was going to be angry something fierce.

But I was having too much fun, so I decided to stay anyway and deal with Daddy tomorrow. I should've sent word so they wouldn't worry, but I just wasn't used to thinking of such things.

Larry invited me out on the porch to talk. It was the first time I'd ever been alone with him. I always kept my sister between us when we sat together in church, but this time there was no one that I could use to keep him away from me.

I was so scared. I could sense that something was different. Maybe it was just because we were alone.

"Bet, come a little closer," he urged as he patted the seat on the porch swing next to him.

Reluctantly, I slowly made my way to the seat next to him. No sooner had I sat down, when he locked

23

eyes with me and leaned in. Wrapping his strong arms tightly around me, his lips latched firmly onto mine.

I'd never been kissed before. It frightened me and at the same time, something in me kind of liked it. I wanted to leave, but I wanted to stay. Conflicted within, I stayed a little longer, but the hugging and kissing continued and my fear began to grow. I pushed him back, "I've got to get some water," I said.

I ran back into the house and grabbed Sally.

"You've got to come out on the porch with me!" I begged Sally. "Please come stay with me so he won't kiss me anymore."

"He kissed you?" Sally smiled. Her eyes widened.

"Yes, but I don't like it," I said.

The two of us returned to the porch together.

"Ya know, I really should be gettin' home. My daddy is gonna kill me."

"Betty, you're exaggerating," Larry replied.

"Am not! Why, I've already seen him whoop my brother nearly to death. One night, Jimmy stayed out all night. He was goin' to leave home. My daddy beat him so bad. He stripped him naked in front of all of us to shame him for what he'd done."

Sally gasped. "Oh, my word."

I continued, "Daddy yelled to the rest of us as we watched, "I'm doin' this to teach you all a lesson. If you leave home, this is what'll happen to you!". I mean to tell you, he whipped him mercilessly."

"You tell your daddy, if he touches you, I'm gonna kill him," Larry said coldly.

I got up the next morning so I could get home and tend to the kids, but I was too late. Daddy was waiting for me in the kitchen.

"Hi Daddy," I said quietly.

"Bet, what did I tell you about leavin' home? It ain't right, a young girl stayin' out all night like that." He reached for his belt.

"I'm sorry, Daddy," I cried.

He started towards me.

"Don't do it, Daddy." Half of me was beggin' him to leave me be, but the other half just had to taunt him. Maybe it was self-preservation that made me tell him what was coming to him if he beat me. "Larry said if you touch me, he is gonna kill you."

"Where's he live?"

I thought for sure Daddy was goin' to kill him. When Daddy left, I took off to town to find my mama.

Running as fast as I could, I finally made it to the doctor's office where she worked. "Mama, come quick!" I yelled, trying to catch my breath.

"Hold on, Bet. What's goin' on? Where have you been?"

"Mama, Daddy is on his way to kill Larry. Come. We've got to stop him."

"Well, honey, Daddy probably thinks Larry has been messin' with you." She tried to reassure me. Then, her head tilted a little to the left. "Bet, has he been messin' with you?"

I thought that trying to kiss you or hug you was messin' with you. I hesitated to answer. I was in so much trouble. I didn't want to die. But Mama would know if I was lyin' and I'd get a beatin' anyway. "Yeah." I answered.

I didn't know nothin' about datin'. I had never dated. Heck, I'd never even had a period and I didn't know what one was either. I'd only turned fifteen two months earlier, and I was quite sheltered from the world. I definitely did not know what sex was. People did not talk about such things. It was considered nasty to talk about it. Mama would surely wash your mouth out with soap if you talked about such things.

We headed home together. Mama had sent for Larry to meet us at the house. Once we arrived, she went in and talked Daddy down while I waited in my room. When Larry arrived, it was time for me to face Daddy.

I could tell he was still really upset. I was scared.

25

"Well, I reckon' it's time for the two of you to get married," Daddy said. "And right away too."

"Tom," Mama said to Daddy, "take 'em up to the preacher tomorrow so as they can git married."

Larry agreed.

After Larry left the house, I begged, "Mama, please. If you won't make me get married, I'll wash the dishes from now on and not complain a bit. Please don't make me get married. I'm afraid."

Mama said, "Bet, you made your bed, now you'll have to lie in it."

When I heard the preacher announce, "You are married. You can kiss the bride." I wanted to run right out that door. But I was too afraid. I was trying to decide if I could outrun Daddy. I knew that he would run right after and stop me, so I stayed put.

I wanted someone to love me, but not like this. In a shotgun weddin', it's the man who's supposed to be afraid, not the woman. But I knew Larry's family was financially much better off than mine. Now, I was free from takin' care of kids and cleanin' the house all the time.

"I'll never go hungry again," I thought to myself.

But freedom is never really free. It always comes with a cost for which someone must atone. I had no idea the price I was about to pay.

5

Becoming a Mama

It was a very small wedding. Daddy was there. Afterall, he had to sign for me to be married, I was too young to do it on my own. But Mama had to work and none of my other kin were there either. My two friends, Sliva and Virginia, dressed me up in their clothes and done my hair. These girls were friends of Larry's, too. I wore a blue suit and a pair of high heels. We never had such things in our mountain home. I felt a little bit like a princess.

My friends were excited that I was marrying Larry. They were raised up with him and they really liked him. All of us sang at church together. I loved singing and getting together to sing with my friends was a lot of fun. But Larry, I didn't like him so much. He looked a lot like a man who lived near us who "wasn't all there". That man always wore a brown derby, same as Larry did, and he would come down by our house to cut wood, just so he could look at me. I was really scared of him. That hat and that suit...ugh! If Larry had dressed like most of the gentlemen that I knew I might have liked him, but to me, he dressed like an old man.

When we got to Larry's house that evening, his mama had a delicious dinner on the table - pork chops and whipped potatoes. . . yum! But there was no party for my wedding. Here I was, I'm a kid, and I'm sitting here next to this old man with a hat and a suit on with his doting mama hovering nearby. It was awkward and uncomfortable.

His brother got killed in a car wreck when he was 20 years old. Larry was the youngest of his siblings, and only a little boy when his brother died. He also had two older sisters and he was his mom's baby. She gave him everything he ever wanted, all his life.

I'd spent my whole life growing up in the country. My new home was now in town and it was much better than what I was used to. It was a cute little white house with a porch that had steps leading down to the street. Upstairs, there were two vacant bedrooms with no furniture in them. Downstairs was the kitchen and dining area.

They would've had a living room, but that's where Larry's parents slept. There was a coal stove in the middle of that room with a few chairs set around it. Larry's mother spent most of her time in bed. She was heavy set with a heart condition. His daddy was a tall, skinny man who loved his chewing tobacco.

Down the hall from the living room was an indoor bathroom. THAT was a very nice change! Much better than the outhouse, I'll tell ya that. Next to that was a bedroom that Larry shared with his brother-in-law, Otis. Otis stayed there during the week to work in the shop. He would go home only on the weekends. Now, I would share a room with both of them.

There were two beds in the room. Larry and I slept in one bed and Otis in the other.

Not only did we have no party to celebrate our new union, but my wedding night would be no fun either. As I entered the bedroom, I was so scared. My heart was beating out of my chest. I'd never been alone with one man. Now, I'd be spending the night in a room with two.

Larry wasted no time. There was no compassion. No warming up. He didn't care that this was my first time. And he gave no mind to having another man being in the room with us. He forcefully took me in such a savage and unloving way. As I cried out in fear and pain, Larry put his mouth over mine, so I couldn't scream. I grabbed onto the bed and tried to get away, but he was much stronger than me. I may not have known what love was, but I was sure it wasn't this.

The next morning, his mother greeted me in the living room.

"Betty, aren't ya going to make your bed?" she asked.

"I can't."

"You can't?"

"The sheets are messed up bad."

She went into the bedroom and came back out. "I thought you said he messed with you." He had told his mom that I told Mama he messed with me, so she thought he had too. Clearly, I didn't know what "messed with you" meant. "You're a virgin?" She sounded surprised.

"What's that?"

"You never had sex before?"

"No, and I don't want to. It hurts!"

Knowing this made her treat me more lovingly after that.

"Here, honey." She handed me the sheets from the bed. "Go soak these in cold water to get the blood out." When I returned, she handed me fresh ones so I could make the bed. But she still didn't explain to me what happened or what my role as wife now was. My mama never explained nothing to me either.

I'd go visit Mama and cry, "Mama, it hurts. I don't want to be married no more."

"I'm sorry," she said, "That's life. You're married now. You have to get used to it."

I hated sex. I hated it with a passion. I hated for nighttime to come.

I wrote to my sister and told her how badly I wanted to go home. She wrote back and told me to go get me some petroleum jelly.

"Petroleum jelly?" I wondered. "What the heck is that?" Man, they threw me to the wolves! Nobody would help me.

I was so naïve and innocent. I just knew nothing of this world and how it worked. Today, that's why I try so hard to help people. I hate ignorance and I do my best to learn so that I can help others learn too. Knowing how to teach yourself is one of the greatest gifts you can give yourself.

I was sixteen when I had my first pregnancy and being with child did not increase Larry's gentleness. He was still a barbaric lover who forced me to have sex even though I didn't want it.

One morning, after a spell of torture in the bedroom, I woke up with blood all over the bed. My husband was at work by this time and I was all alone. I ran to my neighbor next door for help.

"I thought you said you was pregnant," she said.

"Well, I thought I was. But I woke up this morning bloody all over the bed and everything"

She said, "Go over there and tell the preacher across the street. Ask him to take you to the doctor."

Not knowing any better, I followed her advice.

The preacher came to the door. "Can I help you, young lady?"

"I'm about to lose my baby," I said in a panic. "My neighbor told me to come here. I need to go to the doctor. Could you take me?"

The kind preacher had his wife deliver me to the doctor's office. I was so scared. Larry was the only man who'd ever seen me with my clothes off. It was scary having another man lookin' at me, even if it was for the purpose of savin' my life.

"Betty, you just lie still. I'm calling an ambulance to take you to the hospital," the doctor said. "You're bleeding to death. We've got to take this baby."

Out the door he went to go to his desk and call Larry.

I was admitted to the hospital and I was so scared. "Please!" I cried out. "Please take me home."

The doctor and nurse lifted me into bed. Then the doctor gave me a shot. I had never had pain medicine of any kind before that. Seconds later everything seemed to move much slower and my head began to spin.

"Larry get me out of here," I said. "The hospital is turnin' over!"

"No, it's not!"

"Yes, it is! It's goin' around and around and around." I had no idea what was goin' on. All I knew was that I did not want to be there. I tried to get off the bed, but it was like the bed was going to flip. Larry pushed me back down.

"Nurse!" he called out.

The nurse came in to try and calm me down. But it was time to go to the operating room. When I got back to my room there was no more baby.

Three days later, Larry took me home from the hospital and immediately had sex with me again. Every time, from thereafter, every time I had sex with him, I bled.

Before long, I was pregnant again, but I honestly didn't mind. I loved being pregnant because I knew that when my baby was born, I would finally have somebody who loved me.

I was 17 years old when Johnny was born the following spring. He was six pounds and four ounces, and CUTE. They had to take him by forceps which made his head a bit pointy and bruised, but he grew out of it.

Before I had Johnny, I'd never felt loved in my life. But now I finally had someone who loved me. Someone who didn't want me out of his sight. Someone who wanted me to hold him all the time. I was delighted. I had someone who loved me!

I enjoyed nursing my babies. It made me feel loved, wanted and needed. That little baby pulling on my breast and me giving him life, it made me feel good. I held him close.

And Johnny was SMART. By the time he was two, he could tell you the name of every car on the highway. He'd stand behind his daddy as he drove down the road (we didn't have seat belts then).

"There's a Ford, Daddy," he'd say, pointing to the one driving by. "That's a Chevrolet, Daddy." He'd name every one of them.

Men in that day were very proud of having a son, Larry was no different. He spent a lot of time with Johnny.

After Johnny was born, we rented our own house and bought some furniture.

The night that our daughter Peggy came, I nearly died. Larry and his friend, Billy, were there sittin' around pickin' on the guitar when the pains first started.

"Larry," I said. "I think this baby is comin'."

"Aw... nothin' to worry about. That last baby took forever to come out. You've got a while to go. Why don't you walk around a bit?"

I paced the floor for hours and hours. The pain was getting stronger and stronger. "Larry, please...take me to the hospital," I pleaded with him.

"Alright, let me just run Billy home first."

"That's 30 miles away!"

"It'll be ok. I'll be right back."

Larry had no idea how to properly treat a woman or his family. Growing up spoiled, he was all about himself and what he wanted. I was taught to submit to my husband. It was a sin to disobey him.

He left me all alone out in the country, and it was nighttime. Luckily, my son was with my sister-in-law.

I was so scared. I paced the floor crying uncontrollably. I tried and tried to hold that baby in. But the pain got so bad I decided to start walkin' myself to the hospital. As I walked, I prayed that someone would come by and see me, because I was in too much pain. I just wanted to get to the hospital and have that baby. By the time Larry got back and found me walkin' down the road and got me to the hospital, I was slipping into a coma.

"Here ya go, doc." Larry said. "Betty is ready to have her baby. I'll come back later to check on her."

"Wait a minute. You can't go. You've got to stay here and sign papers."

"Why?"

"Because I may have to cut her belly open to get the baby out. She can't help herself now. She's in a coma."

I could hear everything they said. I just couldn't talk. It was like I was between two clouds. You can't move. You can't talk. You can't do anything but lay there. But it was so peaceful to stay there in those clouds.

"Nurse, get me the scalpel."

"Aren't you going to give her something first?"

"She's in a coma. She won't feel it."

But I could feel something. It felt like scissors cutting me down there. But I felt no pain.

"I'm going to break the membranes and see if it will cause her to go into labor. Maybe it'll cause her to open up."

I wasn't opening up to have the baby, even though I'd been in labor for 24 hours. While this was all going on. I started speaking in tongues.

"Oh. She's one of them," the nurse said, "a Holy Roller."

"Don't you EVER," the doctor snapped at the nurse, "say nothing about one of my patients that does this. This is saving her life!"

My doctor always encouraged me about staying with God.

Eventually, they took me down to the labor room where I was able to deliver my daughter with help from the doctor and some forceps.

Peggy was really beautiful. She was seven and a half pounds with jet black hair and big blue eyes. I was excited to have another baby.

Just 6 months after Peggy was born, I was having pain and thought for sure I was having appendicitis, but it turned out I was 3 months pregnant. My daughter, Mary, was so tiny and very sick when she entered this world. She was born premature in my seventh month and weighed only four pounds. She couldn't breathe very well, so they kept her in the incubator and gave her oxygen.

She stayed in the hospital for three months until they couldn't keep her any longer. Then, we took her a hundred miles away to Winston, North Carolina and stayed in a place with the specialist. After evaluating her there, they found that she did not have enough nutrition in the womb. I'd had my babies too fast and much to close together. My body had no time to heal in between. As a result, my baby suffered. I just didn't have enough to give her. In fact, I lost my teeth too. They rotted because the kids were taking all the nutrients from my body. So, at 19 I had all my upper teeth pulled. Mary stayed in the hospital for many more months until she was strong enough to come home.

The worst part of all of that is, I had gotten pregnant again. By the time Mary came home, I'd had another baby, Ann.

Larry made my life a livin' hell. He would rape me every time when I came home from the hospital after havin' my baby. The doctor told me I would die if I had another one.

For my husband to want sex, it was like putting a gun to my head because I thought I would die if I got pregnant again. I was scared to have sex because I was certain I would die. I almost died having every baby.

The doctor told Larry, "If you get her pregnant again, I can't guarantee you she'll survive it."

Yet, once again, I was pregnant with my fifth baby in as many years and once again Larry had forced me to have sex with him. I started hemorrhaging, so he took me to the hospital.

I laid there on the gurney while the doctor interviewed me. His voice was gentle and kind. "Tell me, what happened this morning, Betty?" the doctor asked. "What happened to bring this on? What did you do? Tell me everything you've done."

"Doctor, is it possible that you could be allergic to your husband?"

"What do you mean by that?"

I said, "Well, every time I start hemorrhaging like this, he had sex with me."

"Do you love him?" he asked.

"No."

"Have you ever loved him?"

"No. My daddy made me get married."

The doctor left the room and came back a few moments later with Larry.

"Larry," the doctor said. "Did you know that your wife doesn't love you?"

"Why? What difference does that make?"

"Well," the doctor answered. "It makes a lot of difference if that's what's wrong with her. I think you're abusing her. I'm going to find out. I want you to stay away from her for two weeks. If you don't, she's going to have a nervous breakdown. In fact, she should get away for a few weeks and have some time to herself. No husband. No kids. Just rest."

I went to stay with my sister in Charlotte for those two weeks. While I was away, Larry went to talk to the preacher. I'd only been gone a few days, when Larry and the preacher showed up at my sister's house.

"Betty," the preacher said. "You know, this isn't godly staying away from your husband like this."

"The doctor told me to stay away for two weeks."

"Your husband, he loves you, Betty."

"Come home, Bet," Larry begged.

"No. I don't think I should," I answered. "The doctor told me to rest for two weeks."

"Now, Betty. I know you want to do what's right. And God has made your husband the head of your household. He's telling you to come home. You want to make God happy, don't ya, Betty?"

"Yes, sir."

"Betty, we've got four kids and they need their mama. You've got to come home and take care of them," Larry pleaded.

Inside I knew I wasn't ready, but I obeyed him and returned home.

Within no time, I was back in the hospital, bleeding profusely.

"I want to go home," I cried. "I don't want to be married no more."

"Shhh... it'll be okay, Betty," the nurse whispered.

"I want my mama." I cried and cried. "I want my mama."

"Betty, calm down," Larry said.

"Who are you? Get out of my room!" I shouted at Larry. "I want my mama."

I was delirious. All I wanted was my mama. It was too hard being a grown-up woman. I wanted to be my mama's little girl again.

"Doctor, what's wrong with her?" Larry asked.

"She's having a nervous breakdown," the doctor answered plainly. "I warned you this might happen."

I was just too abused. Too tired. My little body had just been through too much. I just couldn't take it anymore. The thought of enduring more was unbearable. I couldn't think about taking care of the kids and putting up with my husband. I had no future to look forward to. He was spending all of our money. We'd moved every other month, just about. He'd blown what little we had on a new guitar or whatever it was he wanted next. It was a hell of a way to live. It wasn't even that bad at Mama's place.

"She's got the medical history of a forty-year old," the doctor told Larry, "and the body of a teenager."

That's a lot of stress on such a young girl. To have a baby every year, sex every day whether you liked it or not, and mostly I didn't like it, with a husband you don't love...it was just too much.

The doctor saw to it that I was going to get my two weeks of rest one way or the other, so he kept me in the hospital. During those two weeks, they wouldn't let me have any visitors, only my mama.

But eventually she started to agree with Larry. "Bet, you've got you some babies. And they need their mama. You've got to git home and take care of 'em," Mama said. "It's time you snapped out of this."

6

Up in Smoke

While all this was going on, Larry and I were still singing in churches together. Sometimes two times a day. And we sang GOOD. We were sought after. People loved to hear us sing. He had an amazing lead voice and I could harmonize.

Besides my children, God was the only thing I had back then. Preachers would have us come up after service and sing during the alter call.

Softly and tenderly, Jesus is calling
Calling for you and for me
See on the portals He's waiting and watching
Watching for you and for me

I was 20 years old when things started to move for me in the spiritual realm. We would start singing and I said, "We can't close this alter. Someone here is dying tonight. No one can leave here until you know beyond a shadow of a doubt that you're going to heaven."

A man who had been in that service died in his sleep that night. Everybody started to look at me funny. I think it scared me more than it did them. I had been praying for God to give me the gifts of the Spirit. I didn't know what they all were. I only knew about speaking in tongues and interpreting. That's all I'd ever seen in the Church of God. I thought, "God, I'm getting messed up somewhere or another. I'm seeing things and hearing things."

Over time we started five different churches. Larry and I would go start a church and get a hundred people in it and then the Church of God would send a pastor. We would go and rent a building and put flyers out that we were holding meetings there.

Lawrence Carswell was an evangelist that we travelled with. Back then, a lot of churches couldn't afford a full-time pastor, so he would pastor at a different church every Sunday and rotate them. Pastor Carswell would come back every third week to preach. Those churches would still have Sunday school every week and lay people would fill in. Pastor Carswell would pastor Mama's church one week and then travel to two other churches the other weeks. Larry and I travelled with him along with his son, Billy, and his daughter, Dorothy.

We were a quartet. Larry could play all the instruments. He taught Billy how to play the banjo and Dorothy played the piano. Every place we'd go Larry would teach kids how to play the instruments. He was quite good at it. He was so good singing that Nashville had asked him to come, but he turned it down to stay and take care of his family.

After our fifth child, Judy, was born, we were living with Larry's parents again. With two families under the same roof, and all those kids running around, tempers were short. We were like ticking time bombs ready to go off. My marriage was horribly strained, and I couldn't take it anymore. I took my children and we left for a time. We went to live with my sister, and I got a job waitressing.

Larry had no job at that time. He'd come to visit me and the kids, and he'd take all the money I earned each week. Finally, I realized that he was not trying to find a job at all AND I was pregnant again.

A month before my sixth baby was due, Larry got a job and rented a three-room farmhouse for us and I moved back in with him.

We were well into fall and headed toward winter. My sister, Bert, had come over to help me out. She had her little baby with her, too. I wasn't planning to go nowhere that day and being eight months pregnant I did my best to dress comfortably.

All the kids were sleeping on the bed, except Johnny. Bert and I got some kindling from the porch and we started a fire in the wood stove in the front room because it was getting cool out. Johnny, who was five years old, watched us build that fire. Being a young boy, that bright flame intrigued him and, while we cooked dinner, he got him a stick, caught it on fire, and took it into the bedroom where the other kids lay sleeping on the bed. My clothes were hanging to dry on a wire across the room. Johnny touched the flaming stick to the clothes and set them on fire. All the while, Bert and I were in the other room peeling potatoes and cooking dinner. We had no idea this was going on.

Suddenly, my neighbor comes running in the house. Knowing I'm nine months pregnant, she's scared for me to get scared. So, she grabs my hand and calmly says, "Come with me."

I followed her, thinking something was going on outside. Bert followed too. As we get out the front door, she leans over and whispers something to Bert. Then I see Bert run back inside the house, a look of determination on her face.

I still have NO idea what is really going on. I follow my neighbor down to her house. Meanwhile, Bert is throwing the kids out the window to another neighbor who noticed the smoke and ran over to help. By this time, there was no other way out of the house.

As the smoke billowed down the hill to my neighbor's house, I realized what's happening. One by one, my babies were brought to me and I counted them over and over and over again.

We were WAY up in the mountains. Our beautiful little house was surrounded by the woods. Fire trucks couldn't hardly get in. That little wooden house burnt up very quickly. But the firemen were able to get the fire put out before the flames, which had already caught on in the woods, could spread very far.

We may not have had much, but after the fire we had nothing. Nothing at all. Everything we owned had been burned up. Here I was with no bra, no panties on, no shoes – just a maternity skirt and a top.

I was taken to the hospital, because I was right out of my mind. "One's missing! One's missing!" I'd scream and then start counting my babies all over again. Eventually, they got me to calm down. My babies were not harmed. I was ok. Somehow, everything would work out.

The next day, we were headline news in our local paper. Belk department store sent a bathrobe, gown, and slippers to the hospital, so I'd have something to wear when I went home. The furniture store sent over two sets of bunk beds and a bedroom suite. We got a brand-new refrigerator and stove. Churches came and brought us food, groceries, and money. You name it, boy. We thought we was rich! We were the best off that we'd ever been. That fire may have been the best thing that ever happened to us.

Weeks later, Cheryl was born. I was in labor for days and the doctor had to take the baby out before he lost both of us.

I was in the hospital for two weeks this time. When I left, I was still incredibly weak. Thankfully, people brought us baby clothes. Then, for Christmas, the fire trucks came again. This time, with ALL kinds of stuff for us. They brought us a REAL BIG sugar-cured country ham with all the fixin's, tricycles, toys—all kinds of stuff.

We were married six years with six kids. I believed that Larry would stay married to me forever. But my husband grew strangely cold toward me.

After Cheryl was born, I'd had surgery and was weak and spent most of my time lying in bed. There was no way I could travel and sing in churches with Larry in this condition. Eventually, Larry had grown sweet on one of the girls at our church. I didn't know this until her mother came to the house one day.

"I'm sorry, Betty. I don't approve of this, but I've done everything I can."

"What are you talking about?" I asked.

"Why my daughter and Larry, they've been seeing each other."

That's how I found out that my husband was with another woman. Over the years, he'd teased me that someday he would replace me with a younger girl. I had been sick and in hospitals so much that he finally did just that.

I don't think I really cared that he was seeing other women. I hated having sex with him and I was glad someone else would do that now. But, being left was hard for me to accept. I thought you got married for life. Whether it was good or bad, you stayed married. That's just how it was. "You made your bed, now lie in it." That's what Mama and Daddy would say.

But Larry, was lying in another women's bed now – a younger woman.

I was now with six kids and no way to support them. Larry left for another city – just disappeared one day. I didn't know where he was at, only that he was with someone else.

A woman at church got me a job at the cotton mill and my little sister, Lyda, came and stayed with me to take care of the children. She was about 13 years old. She loved my kids and took good care of them. In exchange, I'd buy her new school clothes. She loved that!

While working in the factory one day, I hurt myself reaching up for a large barrel of yarn. I slipped three discs and fractured my spine doing that and ended up in the hospital yet again.

It had been at least a year since I'd heard from my husband. While I was in the hospital he showed up and took all the furniture.

At the hospital, they put me in a steel brace (that the factory refused to pay for) and I couldn't walk without it. I definitely couldn't work now. So, I had no choice but to go back to Mama and Daddy's. But times were tough for them, too.

I was barely a week out of the hospital, lying on a pallet Mama had put down on the floor for me and my babies to sleep on, when Daddy came in with his decision.

"Betty," Daddy said, "I want you to know this is what a man can do for you. You shouldn't have been workin' in no factory. That's man's work. Learn your lesson."

I was in pain and so scared of what Daddy was going to say next.

"I'm gonna go to town and I'm gonna have the welfare department come and take your kids. You're not able to take care of 'em and we're not going to either."

After Daddy left, I got my brother to help me up and asked him to take me to Larry. I'm in a brace, with six kids, going to find my husband. It was 2:00 pm when we arrived at his house. Remember, he was living with this other woman now. He was at work and she was home alone. She invited us in, and we all sat in the living room until he came home.

The surprised look on his face brings joy to me now, but it was clear then that he was not happy to see me. He was happy to see the kids, though. He went into the kitchen with his girlfriend, so they could talk. Moments later, he loaded me and the kids into his car and took me over to this house and moved my furniture in. He didn't put it away or nothin'. He just left it there in the middle of the room and went back home.

7

Ignorance is Mean

The children and I went without a lot of things. There were times when we had no electricity. Many times, we had no food. But I was proud, AND I was afraid that if I let anyone know that we had needs that the Welfare Department would come and take my children away.

My next-door neighbor's daughter worked at the factory right up the street from us. She talked to her boss who, having a sister that was paralyzed, felt sorry for me and gave me a job in his fiberglass plant.

Inside the plant, there were these large marbles, the size of a shooter marble, that came down from the ceiling and it would go around and around and around making fiberglass thread wrapped around a large spindle. Then they brought it to me where I would spin it on this round thing, and I would have to get all the loose glass off of it. From me, it went to another area where it would be woven into sheets of fiberglass and it would eventually become strong materials for missiles. Even though I didn't have to move around very much, it was hard. Fiberglass would get all in my hands and bleeding was normal. Still, I was able to sit there on that little stool with that brace on and make money. I worked that job and stayed there for three years.

Now, this boss man of mine, James, was GOOD lookin' AND he had a band. His mom and sister were on disability and he didn't have a car, so I let him borrow my car to take his sister to the doctor. And sometimes he would use it to take his mom to buy groceries, too. In a short period of time, we became good friends and eventually he became my boyfriend.

Finally, I learned what love was really like. I learned that sex could be good, though I wasn't married to James. My young mind was not fully committed to living the way that God wanted me to live. I was so hungry for love. I didn't understand that no man would ever be able to love me the way that Jesus can. I only knew that, for once, I felt loved, and it felt awesome.

I was still legally married to Larry, but we'd been separated for quite a while with no intentions of getting back together. Back then, you had to be separated for two years before a judge would grant a divorce. Larry and his pregnant girlfriend were living at his mom and dad's place.

One day, James came to look for me. I didn't show up for work and he was worried. I never missed a shift. He found me passed out on my bed in a pool of blood. I was hemorrhaging from my uterus. He called the ambulance and I went to the hospital and had a D&C again.

After that, I'd be at work and just start bleeding out of nowhere. I often didn't even realize it was happening until it would come through my clothes and someone would notice.

"Betty, this has happened several times," James said. "It's embarrassing, and the other workers are really bothered by it. You've got to do something about this or I'm going to have to let you go."

I was standing at the employment line the next day. Suddenly, I heard this pop sound go off deep in my belly and I felt this explosion on the inside of me. Instantly, blood was running down my legs. A worker came running with a towel and put it between my legs, but it wasn't enough. In seconds it was soaked through.

"Honey, you got to get to the hospital, FAST," she said to me. "You're hemorrhaging."

I ran out, jumped in my car, and drove myself to the hospital just as fast as I could. When I got to the hospital, I walked right in. "I'm bleeding to death," I said as I dropped to the floor, passed out. They rushed me straight into an emergency room suite. For three days they packed me and gave me blood, trying to get me strong enough for surgery.

"Doctor, she's bleeding just as fast as we put it in," the nurse said.

There seemed to be no hope for me. Then Mama and some church folks got there and prayed for me.

I had a complete hysterectomy at 23 years of age. That's enough to drive a girl crazy they say. Nobody can't believe that it didn't. And I ain't never took no hormones. I made up my mind that it was a lie what they say about it. I was young and I decided I liked sex, and I'm gonna have sex. I don't have to worry about getting pregnant. I'm gonna enjoy myself. And I enjoyed sex. I loved sex. It felt good. And they say you're not supposed to enjoy it after, that's hogwash. It's up to your mindset. Women believe in that lying spirit and then they get cold.

Ya know what helped me with that? I got on an elevator one day and there was a nurse on there with me and I was havin' a hot flash.

"Just think like this," she said. "Your body is going from creation and having babies and now it's going to totally change. Your mind is tellin' you, 'We aren't goin' to get pregnant anymore and we aren't goin' to have babies. We don't need to produce milk no more.' Everything is changing. It's all changing so just ignore it."

47

That helped me more than anything else. So, when I'd get those feelins I'd just say to my body "Oh, you're just changing."

Your body does whatever your mind is thinking. So, just do what I do and tell your body, "This body is full of the Holy Ghost. There ain't no room for that here!"

In order for me to have that surgery, the law had to go get Larry and make him come and sign the papers. They told him they'd put him in jail if he didn't.

"I can't believe the law would have to make you come and sign these papers," James yelled at Larry.

"What good is a woman if she can't have babies?" Larry asked.

"She's dyin' if she don't have it."

"Well, she wouldn't want to live if she can't have babies."

James would've liked to whoop him. Finally, fearing the threat of jail, Larry signed them.

I was in the hospital for a month. James' mom took care of my children while I was recovering and my next-door neighbor, who was my babysitter, helped. When I finally emerged from the hospital, Elsie, my babysitter had my kids. She told me that the welfare department had been by and said they was going to take them because I couldn't take care for them.

"Let me take 'em. Give me some time to get away before you call 'em back," I begged. Elsie agreed.

I scooped up my babies, loaded them in the car, and went to Mama's.

The welfare department was waiting on me to bring the children to them. Mama went to talk with them, and they agreed that when I was better, they would give the babies back to me. What I didn't know at the time was that I was not expected to live. I had cancer. Nobody told me. Back then, they told the family, but not the patient.

So, Mama talked me into giving the children to Larry until I was better. He even agreed that I could have them back when I got better.

I thought I was going to get better and get my children back. They all thought I was dying. I had no idea.

In court, the judge gave Larry full custody. We had been separated for three years. He never even bothered to visit them. Now, my babies were going to live with a daddy who was like a stranger to them.

I had lost everything.

Well, I didn't die. I got better. So, I made a plan to get out of the jurisdiction of the North Carolina welfare so I could eventually steal my kids. To keep them, I'd have to get them out of North Carolina. I went to Georgia and James followed me there.

In Georgia, I couldn't find nothing but waitress jobs. And I wasn't strong enough to do those. Because of all my health problems, I had to find a job that didn't involve physical labor.

James found a job managing a hotel and so I went to work for him. It wasn't long before an even better opportunity came along.

"Betty, I've got a chance for a really good promotion if I go to Dallas, Texas. Do you want to go?"

I said, "Yeah!"

In time, I was able to get a job managing a hotel too. Now, I had a new boss. This man was the owner of the hotel that I managed. Within six months, I had enough money saved and I was motivated to leave James and go back and get my kids.

I thought for sure Larry and his girlfriend would easily give them back to me, but they had no intentions. The last thing they wanted to do was have to pay me child support. Larry had already paid me child support in the past – a whopping $30 that he begged me to have lowered to $15 a week to raise six kids! He did not want to return to that. Their problem was not that they did not want me to have my kids. The problem was they did not want to have to pay me child support.

Fully recovered, I returned to get them back anyway.

Larry's girlfriend was really pregnant by this time. Here I was thin with long black hair – gorgeous. She took one look at me and jealousy got the best of her. She did not want me around her "husband". Even though we'd been apart for quite some time, he still always called me Honey. He'd called me that all my life. He never called me Betty. Honey was my name as far as he was concerned, and his girlfriend hated me for that. Pulling up in my beautiful, white Lincoln convertible didn't make her love me anymore either, I'll tell you that. My boss at the time gave me quite the deal on that Lincoln. He was getting divorced and didn't want his ex-wife to have it. He knew that I needed a car to go out and do his business, so he sold it to me real cheap.

Several of my children were playing in the front yard, when I pulled up. I was so happy to see them. I got out of the car and they swarmed me. Hearing their little voices sing out, "Mommy! Mommy!" just about made my heart burst with joy.

As I approached the house, the front door swung open and Larry's girlfriend was standing there with a shotgun pointed straight at me.

"Where's Larry?" I asked.

"Leave! If you come in, I'll shoot you."

I got back in my car and drove directly to the Sherriff's Department.

"What can I do?" I asked the deputy.

"You have to hire a lawyer. There is nothing we can do for you," he answered.

I decided to look for Larry at the service station where he'd occasionally hang out with his buddies. The service station wasn't only a place where you could buy gasoline for your car. It was also where the town mechanic worked on cars. There was a small waiting area inside of the station. In those days, it was totally normal for a man to go down to the station and have a cup of coffee, shoot the breeze with his friends and hang out together in that little waiting area – even if their car wasn't being fixed.

His girlfriend was already there to tell him I was in town. I saw her walking toward him as I pulled into the lot. I was so angry and so hurt. Something inside whispered to my mind that she was the only thing between me and my children and now I was able to do something about that.

I went for it, aimed my car at her and pressed down on the accelerator. Larry jumped between us and put his hands up.

"Whoa! Honey, stop!"

Looking back, it seems odd that I wasn't even more motivated to run him over instead, after all he'd put me through. But he was the father of my children and my love for them and knowing they needed their daddy forced me to slam on the brakes.

"Get out of my way, Larry. She's keeping me from my kids and I'm gonna kill her!"

"Please. Please just calm down and think about this. That ain't gonna solve nothin'," he pleaded with me.

Suddenly, I snapped out of it. Realizing how close I'd come to doing something so horrible scared me so much. I just took off down the road and waited for another opportunity to get my kids.

I don't recall how, but I finally got all my kids in the car and took off on highway 321. Larry came after me. When he caught up to me, he pulled his Oldsmobile right up next to my Lincoln. Screaming and yelling for me to pull over, his anger took over and he ran my car off the road right into the ditch.

Larry jumped from his car and began pulling the kids from the back door.

"Come on, get out!" he yelled at them.

He came to my window and began punching me over and over in the head. Then he grabbed hold of my shirt so forcefully that it tore. His fist cocked back to hit me once again, "Don't you ever try this again!" His eyes threatened. The kids' crying seemed to pull him away. Larry jumped back in his car and drove off with them.

We were right across from the service station and the man there saw everything and called the law. Soon after, Larry was sitting in the jail house behind bars.

A few days later, we were in the courthouse. The judge was prepared to send Larry to prison for what he'd done to me. If I'd had any sense, right there is where I could've asked for custody of my kids. In fact, I could have sent him off too. But I still had enough God in me, "How could I tell my children that I sent their daddy to prison? That's the father of my children. How can I let him go to prison?" I asked myself.

"Your honor," I said, "He's the father of my children. I don't want him to go to prison. I just want to see my children."

"You two get out of my courtroom," he said in disgust, "and don't you ever come back."

Ignorance is mean. I hate it. That's why I teach Bible school. Ignorance messed up my life and it messed up my kids' lives. I think everybody should be educated. At least about the law and definitely about the Bible. No one was ever there to help me. Now, I couldn't even seem to help myself.

When my husband first left me, I was alone taking care of six kids and no one helped me. Not one church member brought me food. No one visited me. Not one encouraged me – not even the pastor. As far as they were concerned, I couldn't keep a husband and that made me a disgrace. Even now, it's still a little that way in North

Carolina. If you do wrong, they ain't forgiving you. In their eyes, I was a hussy.

I returned to my job in Texas to save more money. I was determined that one day I would finally be back with my babies for good.

Weeks later, I got a call from a friend at the fire department back at home. He let me know that they were letting Johnny run around at night in the pool rooms and all. He was only 8 years old! I was so afraid that somebody would attack him or hurt him in some way. The man at the fire department told me that if I would pay for a bus ticket, he'd send Johnny to live with me. So, I did right away. At least I had one of my children with me now.

8

Show Business

A month or two later, a friend of mine says, "Hey Betty, let's go to Atlanta."

"Ok," I said, willing to give it a try.

She was much more experienced in the world than I. You should have seen me when I saw Atlanta for the first time. It was such a big city. Me, I'd hardly even been to town much in my life let alone a big city like that. It scared the heck out of me. I tried to work as a waitress. She and I had both had experience waitressing in North Carolina. My legs and feet would swell so bad from all those hours standing. I just couldn't do it. I decided I was going to be a country music singer.

Someone told me about The Nightery, a swanky club that everyone in the city went to. It was so fancy that a man in a top hat stood outside the club every night and escorted people in.

They were accepting auditions for their variety show. The show featured a country music duet, a comedian who comes out and tells jokes, and then they would have new people come and perform as well. It was a big production. On each side of the stage go-go dancers, dressed in fringe, would dance away.

I was excited to sing again, and some friends told me I sounded like Patsy Cline, so I went to try out. This woman who owned the place had been raised by Pentecostals, so she knew all about me, maybe even more than I did. She eyed me up and down. I knew she was checking me out, but I wasn't sure why.

"Here honey, let me give you a drink." She poured me a vodka Collins. "It tastes just like Mama's lemonade," she smiled assuring me. It was good. She poured me another. And then another. "Here, just drink this and relax," she told me.

After I'd finished those drinks, she said, "I'll tell ya what. I'll give you a job go-going."

"What's that?" I asked.

She had a couple girls go up next to the stage and dance so I could see.

"I'll pay ya $150 a week to be a go-go dancer."

"$150?" I thought to myself. "I can't even make $60 a week doing most kinds of work." Even secretaries couldn't make that.

"Now wait a minute. I can't even be alone in a room with the opposite sex without feeling ashamed and awkward. And you want me to go up there and dance in front of everybody?"

The devil whispered into my ear. "They're right. You're not a fit mother. A real mother would do anything to get her kids back. If you were a real mother, you'd go up there and do that and go back and get those kids."

Finally, I got so mad. "I'll show you I can do it!"

I'd had a few drinks, so I was feeling a lot braver than usual. But once I got up there, memories of me singing in front of church flooded my mind and washed all the club people away. Tears streamed down my face as I danced my way into my new job.

The entire time, all I could think about was my babies. I didn't want to do this, but I had no choice. I was broken and ashamed, but I'd learn to ignore that. A mama has got to do what she's got to do. Fortunately, I was good at dancing.

Eventually, it bothered me so bad that I had to get on Valium just to do it. Those pills and the drinking every night just so I could dance could've killed me. I didn't realize it at the time. That is exactly what the devil wanted to do – kill me. One way or the other, he had to take me down... one step at a time.

A year or so later, the owner approached me again. It was time for a promotion.

"Betty, if I give you a gown and you take it off, I'll raise your pay to $500 a week."

$500 a week? Money talks. I couldn't turn it down. I'd be rich! I could surely get all my babies back then.

By today's standards, most of America wouldn't think it was all that bad. What they call bikinis nowadays is what we ended up in. In the 1960s, however, it was quite provocative – definitely not how I was raised to be. Things they do today, in public even, like wearing a G-string to show your behind. We'd be arrested in our club for that. But I had to make a living. I had my six children to support. I had to do something to provide for them so I could get them back.

I started out doing high kicks and the kinds of modest moves I learned to do in dance class at school. Over the years, I got more sensuous, taking my stockings off and such.

The life of a stripper is more like "normal" people than you'd guess. By day I was an everyday mom. I dressed like all the other moms. I went to the grocery and did all the things that other moms did. You'd never know what I did for a living based on how I lived my life in the daytime. My other life didn't start until 10:00 at night. My little Johnny was asleep in bed when I went off to work. And I'd leave the club around 6:00 in the morning, so he never knew I was gone. My kids never knew what I'd done. My family didn't even have any idea what I was doing for a living. I did my best to keep it from everybody. That's why I stayed so far away from home so no one would figure out what I'd done.

My work "day" consisted of quite more than just dancing. Us girls would arrive through the side door in disguise with sunglasses, no makeup. We didn't want anyone to recognize us and follow us home later on. Once inside, I went to my dressing room to put on my makeup and get myself all dolled up for customers. I didn't dress for the show just yet. Us dancers would wear something sexy, like a mini skirt or something so that men would want to visit with you and buy you a drink. We made great bonus money selling drinks. Above all, you never use your real name. This was show business and with it came your stage name and the fake ID to go with it. My name (in the club) was now Vickki Lee.

A typical night would go something like this: As the men entered the club, they would choose a girl to drink with and the hostess would come over to each of us, once selected, and say, "Number so and so would like to buy you a drink."

"Hello," I smiled flirtatiously.
"Have a seat, darlin'. What would you like to drink?"

"Oh, let's party and have a bottle of champagne," I'd say.

I earned $25 from the club right there. Basically, I was a pusher of drinks —a hustler who got paid at the end of the night for the number of drinks I sold. Inside every drink, the bar tender puts a stir in it. I collected those stirs and turned them in at the end of the night and I'd get money for each one. I'd "drink" with several dozen men a night.

Generally, the gentleman would drink the booze. I was "drinking" champagne. Now, let's be real, there's no way I could drink a couple dozen drinks every night. We were taught how to do this so that the men never knew that we weren't really drinking. Not that much anyway.

When the hostess would seat the men, she would have him scoot to the inside of the booth and us girls would sit on the outside. I'd place the bucket of ice on the ground next to me, pour myself a glass of champagne, and then place the bottle back into the bucket upside down. Then, I'd sip on my drink. Meantime, I'm ordering him one drink after another until he was drunk. After three drinks, he'd be cut off and they'd make him leave.

I learned really quick that you are there making your money as fast as you can. I averaged hundreds of dollars a night just in booze sales.

Sometimes, the men would be a little smarter. They'd get a drink and say, "Now I want to make sure you drink this."

So, I'd get a shot of booze and a glass of water to go with it. I put the shot in my mouth, then I'd take a "sip of water" and slowly let all that booze out of my mouth and into the glass of water. I had all sorts of tricks.

Of course, a lot of that time was talking with the guys and building them up, telling them how awesome they are.

I'd grab their muscles and say, "Boy, your wife must really like you." I'd tell them everything they wanted to hear. That's why they come in there. They come in to get built up and go home and have sex. Dancing was such a small part of my job. I spent most of my time just chatting with fellas. I only danced 3 times a night, at most.

I learned that the wives were not telling them what they needed. And what I was giving them was confidence. They did not come in there wanting to have sex with us. Their wives would not turn them on. These men like black garters, stockings, push-ups and all. When we got up there in those get ups, they'd hit the door, ready to go home and have sex with their wives. They loved it so much they would pay me $50 to wear a red bra and panties and dance in them.

I'd tell the men who wanted to talk to me that I had six kids and I was trying to make a living to support them. "If you want to talk to me and you want to buy me a drink, that's great. But don't waste my time. It's going to cost you."

I know. I know what you're thinking. "But Betty, you didn't have all six kids living with you then."

I was a professional liar. Everything I told those men was a lie. Typically, I told them what they wanted to hear.

Most of the gals I worked with would do things I'd never do. And they were mean as hell to me. They were all there to just make a living. A lot of them were older. I was the youngest one. The oldest one was in her seventies. Under the lights with the makeup and all, you don't look as old as you are. And there were a number of lesbian women who worked as dancers too. They worked there because they liked women. They could sit there and lust after you and get paid to do it.

You see the worst of everybody in a place like that. Even people I knew, friends, their husbands, police, ministers and priests. Sooner or later, it seemed like they all came into the club and many tried to proposition me to have sex for money.

Eventually, Larry divorced me. He claimed he had tried to notify me but couldn't find me and that is when he got permanent custody of the kids.

I was now in my early thirties, living in Missouri for a period of time. I gave up dancing and I worked in a hotel. One day, I came home to North Carolina for a family reunion. My sisters greeted me when I arrived. It was so good to be with family again.

59

"Larry's over at the park playing ball," Bert said. "Go on over there, sis, and see the kids."

My new boyfriend was with me. We pulled up to the park in my convertible. The kids saw me and came running. They were climbing in the car and hugging on me and loving me. Of course, Larry came over and started talking with me as he pulled the kids out of the car one by one. My little Judy was sitting on my lap.

"Judy! Come on now," Larry called to her.

"I don't want to get out, Daddy." She whined and wrapped her little arms tightly around my neck and she started hugging on me like you can't believe. I carried a .38 special with me back then. It was sitting right close, in my purse.

Larry's new wife said to me, "You lost all rights to your kids. You're not fit to be a mother."

Of all the people to say that to me. I done wanted to kill her once before. She ought to know better. I reached down to grab my purse. My boyfriend saw and he knew exactly what I was doing. He threw that car in gear and floored the gas pedal. Larry jumped back.

Larry had gotten all the other kids out, but I realized, "Oh my God! I got Judy! I got Judy!"

"What do you want me to do?" my boyfriend asked.

"Go home! Go home!" I squealed with delight.

We returned to Atlanta with my sweet little girl. I was afraid to go back to North Carolina for fear they'd arrest me for kidnapping. But I eventually learned that Larry did not report me. As long as I didn't ask for child support, he was going to let me be.

But my other babies were left feeling like they weren't good enough. Their dad and his wife convinced them that I didn't want them. It stayed this way for years.

Peggy eventually came to live with me when she was fifteen. Ann called when she was fifteen, too, and wanted me to come get her. So, I went and got her. Then

Mary called and said she was sick, and she wanted to come stay with me for a month. Cheryl was such a small child when I'd lost custody that she really didn't even know me. She knew about me, but she didn't really remember being with me. The opportunity to bond as mother and child had long since passed, or so I thought.

When she was a teenager, she had a supernatural encounter with Jesus. Afterwards, she reached out to me. I was living in Miami at that time.

"Mama," Cheryl said, "I don't really know you. But I know you're my mother and I love you. And I want to come and see you. I want to get to know you."

We've been close ever since.

Finally, my babies had all returned.

9

Love Comes Calling

I originally moved to Miami wooed by my boyfriend and his promises of a beautiful life. It was anything but beautiful. I had three of my kids living with me by this time, but I had to return to dancing just to make ends meet. Eventually, I left this dead beat and went back to being on my own.

"I don't need no man to enjoy my life," I told myself.

Love seemed to escape me no matter how I tried to pursue it. It was time I tried a new strategy. I didn't really think of it that way at that moment. I just needed to protect myself and I needed to protect my children.

The club I worked at in Miami was high class. Our clients were senators, congressmen, all sorts of people who run the country. Most of my customers were prosperous. We had a very special clientele. Frank Sinatra and Dean Martin used to come into our little French review, Place Pical. It was world famous.

I was the star of the show and my name was in great big lights on the marquee: Vickki Lee, Satan's Angel, the Devil's Own Mistress.

Being in Miami did have lots of perks. Beaches and boats were the norm for most folks on Miami Beach. I was no different. I loved sunning myself on the deck of a boat and I did so as often as I had a chance. One day I was out with some friends on a fishing boat. I had a bikini on and got right up on the bow so I could get sun. I got so burned that day. That night in the club, everyone noticed my new red glow. Even in the dim lights it was quite noticeable.

There was this wealthy man named George who would come in and easily spend $1,000. He was one of our biggest clients. I noticed him because he would wear white shirts, cuffed up like my brothers and my daddy and it made me homesick. His face was smooth as silk and his blonde, Danish hair was so shiny and beautiful. He was over six feet tall. I generally liked brown-eyed, black-haired men, but there was something about this man that captivated me.

He captivated the other women in the club, as well. I shook my head as night after night these sleezy women would take advantage of him. Here he was spending all kinds of money and these girls was really playing him. I wasn't one of the girls he was buying drinks for. I had my own set of clients.

One night, I was sitting with George's nephew in one booth and George and a lesbian girl was in the next one. Of course, he didn't know she was gay or that she was a hooker. But I knew it.

He was on one side of the booth. His prostitute friend on the other side. She wasn't that pretty in the face, but she did have a great figure. Being a hooker, she wasn't snuggling up to no man. Our heads were back to back and I could hear everything he said. His "date" opened up the champagne, and every time I heard the cork, I'd lean back, turn my head slightly and whisper, "Sucker."

Every time he came to the club, I'd walk by his table, bend down to his ear and say, "Sucker."

I was mean. For some reason, I wanted to tease him about how badly he was being taken, lured by a woman who had no interest in men. Because he reminded me of my family, I just wanted him to go home. I wanted to protect him even though he was a grown man who didn't need my protection.

He liked my mean tease. It got his attention. And though I didn't notice him that day, he had already noticed me the day I came in with the sunburn.

One night, George said to me, "You think you are so smart. I'm going to see how smart you are." He lined up ten shots of Cutty Sark on the table. "You're gonna drink these," He challenged with a seductive smile on his face.

I drank every one of them.

"I gotta go pee," I said.

I went to the bathroom and made myself throw up. Then, I went back out to George.

"Line 'em up again." We laughed and George lined up ten more shots. I wasn't going to let him get me.

Its dog eat dog out there. You're out there for one purpose and one purpose only. Mine was to come out with money to take care of my children. That was it. I made up my mind. "The booze and the drugs ain't getting to me because I don't trust 'em. I'm using this job for one purpose. I'm going to control it. It ain't gonna control me."

My brother, Truman, had taken ill and he was in the hospital. I wanted so badly to get home. George and I had become great friends. When he heard about my brother, he called me.

"Betty, you should go home and be with your family."

"I can't afford to. And besides, I ain't got nobody to leave Judy with."

"I'll fly yins up there," George said. "Go to the counter at the airport. I'll have a ticket waiting for you. And I'll have a car waiting on you to rent. I'll pay for it all."

I arrived home in North Carolina, relieved that I'd be able to spend time with my brother and the rest of my family. Then, I found out that George had flown in too and he was in a hotel there.

One night, he took all my sisters, me, and my cousin out dancing. I had on a pretty, black jumpsuit. George was a terrific dancer. He loved to waltz, and he led me around the dance floor like a prince. We all had a ball. George was buying everyone drinks and all my sisters and cousins were sitting around chatting with him. Me and my brother Bob was dancing. Then, they asked me to sing. When I got through, I jumped off the stage and did a high kick and then the splits and everyone in the place wanted to dance with me after that. They ain't never seen nothing like that in North Carolina.

Years later, George told me, "When you did that. I said to myself, 'That's mine.'"

When it was time to go back home, George traveled with Judy and me. We went down to Charlotte to stay in a hotel so we could catch a plane the next morning. George and I slept together that night.

When I woke the next morning, the sudden realization of what I'd done shocked me. You see, in the club he was always looking nice. Even though he was ten years older than me, I was still attracted to him. But waking to his teeth in a cup next to the bed was a bombshell I didn't expect. I was used to Mr. Texas and all these hunks that I dated for years. Now, I'm with an old man!

After we returned to Miami, I went to my boss at the club, "If George comes in, you tell me," I instructed her. Well, she didn't tell me. He sat back in the club watching as I'm goofing off and flirting with other men

65

— doing things that I didn't want him to see. After the way he'd treated me so well on our trip to North Carolina, I'd made up my mind that I wanted him. When I realized he was there, I got so mad.

"You were supposed to tell me if George came in. Why didn't you tell me? I quit!"

"Go ahead, quit," my boss said to me. "But I ain't paying you."

George overheard our argument. He was there with a friend and hearing this upset him. "You aren't going to pay her? We'll see about that." He and his friend began to tear the place apart. Tables were flipping and next thing I knew I was out of the club business.

I lived with George for about a year, and we eventually got married. George was so proud of me. When he'd introduce me to people, he'd say, "I'd like you to meet my wife," with such endearment. It made my heart smile. He was so good to me and I fell madly in love with him. I'd never had anybody treat me as well as he did.

Imagine my surprise when I started to realize just how miserable I was without my show business career. I missed being the center of the universe. Having all those men fall all over me made me feel special.

"What's wrong with me?" I asked myself.

By 10:00 a.m. every day, I wanted a drink.

George tried to please me and bought me a whole case of champagne. Whenever I felt bad, I'd just have drink. He had been in the service and had his own battle with alcohol in his younger years.

He said, "Honey, you got a problem."

"No, I don't!" I'd cuss at him for saying I had a problem.

"I'm going to let you go back. At least when you're dancing you don't drink. And you pride yourself in your show. That's the only way you're going to be able to control this. But if you're going to go back, you're going to go big and you're going to be the best."

So, he bought me a brand-new wardrobe and I had professional photos taken. Then, we bought a big, new sixty-foot motor home with a king size bed and everything I needed to travel in comfort. I got myself a booking agent who booked me for shows all over the United States. We'd moved to Dallas and I was now Vickki Lee from the Big D. I danced at supper clubs, conventions, and all kinds of big shindigs. Before long, I was booked in Vegas. I was famous!

We decided we were going to move to Vegas. But first, I needed to get myself a little "enhancement."

I'd noticed that all the dancers I knew were having their breasts enlarged, and decided I needed mine done too. I chose a surgeon who had done this type of surgery on many movie stars.

"Doctor," I said, "I want my breasts to be size 42C."

He laughed. "Well, I can make that happen for you if it's what you really want."

George had no objections to the cost.

The doctor had a surgical suite right there on the premises. They didn't even use general anesthesia, just a local and some sedatives. I was awake when the surgery started. Unbeknownst to the doctor, I'd lied a teeny bit on my intake forms. Someone had told me they'd never do this surgery if they knew I had a history of being a bleeder and I knew best not to tell him I'd had a drink or two the night before.

I was heavily sedated and really out of it when the doctor made the first cut. It felt as though something landed on my face. I opened my eyes to see blood covering the doctors face and glasses.

The devil whispered in my ear, "See there. That's your blood. That's what you get for lying to your doctor. You lie to everyone and now you are going to die," said the greatest liar to ever walk the face of the earth.

The doctor was able to control the bleeding and finished the surgery. It was supposed to be a simple procedure, but my half-truths and lies made it a much bigger deal. Still, I was able to go home that day, as long as I promised to take good care of myself.

Wouldn't you know . . . I ended up with a horrible infection since I'd been opened up so long, because of my bleeding. I went to the doctor for an injection of penicillin every single day – had to for five days. But day four the nurse noticed an ugly red mark at the injection site.

"Doctor, will you take a look at this?" The nurse asked.

"Hmmm."

"Maybe we shouldn't give that to her anymore. Looks like a reaction."

"Let's try one more day," the doctor directed.

The next day was Thanksgiving and the doctor's office would be closed. So, the nurse taught George how to give me my last shot.

As Thanksgiving Day began, I was so appreciative of the life I'd built. I looked at my children, my husband, and this glorious career I had in show business. I was booked in Vegas and touring the United States as a star in my luxurious motor home, what more could any girl want?

Smiling, I thought to myself, "I have achieved EVERYTHING."

Little did I know, that at four o'clock that evening I'd be in eternity. We don't know. We have no idea when our time is going to be up.

10

To Hell & Back

That Thanksgiving Day, in 1974, will be forever marked in my memory.

After eating that delicious turkey and all the trimmings, the children settled in front of the television. George and I went into our bedroom.

I hugged him around the neck and rubbed up against his body.

"George, honey," I said all sweet and suggestively, "give me my shot so I can take a shower." I proceeded to tease and give him a little show as I undressed. George took out the syringe and drew up the penicillin while I danced.

I backed my bottom toward him. I knew he liked that and pleasing him made me happy. Finally, he had the shot ready. I bent over towards the nightstand. As I felt the needle pull out of me, I felt this strange sensation rushing up my spine. It went up my neck and across my jaw. I felt myself go limp as lights of all colors and brightness flashed before my eyes. And I heard these weird, loud noises like a combination of sirens and rushing winds. As I fell to the ground, I heard that awful voice once again, "This time, you are going to die."

Our physical body is just like clothing. When you leave this world, you "unzip" your suit and just slide right out of it. In my spirit body, I could still see and hear my family. My memory was fully intact. I could recognize and name each one of them.

"Kids!" George screamed. "Get in here! Your mama needs help!"

My children entered the bedroom. My naked body lay still on the bed. A black silhouette of a man grabbed my arm.

"Satan, let go of me!" I yelled.

Your spirit is a full person inside of you and your spirit body is a real body. You have arms and legs, and you can feel. Satan was sitting next to me at the edge of the bed. His cold hand grabbed onto my arm and pulled me from my body. Then he dragged me to the other side of the room.

When you are out of your body, you are unclothed. You no longer have what protected you. That is why demons want so badly to get into you. They have no body of their own. Not only can you feel physical feelings, but you have emotions as well. I was so scared.

My husband picked up the phone to call for an ambulance. I felt helpless as I watched my family desperately trying to save me.

"Rub your mother so she won't lose her brain! She's in trouble. Rub her all over. Every one of ya, rub her!" George yelled.

Frantically, the children began to rub my arms and legs.

"Wake up, Mama!"

I looked at the devil. "Satan, you told me that I'd just go to sleep. You told me there is no hereafter. You lied to me!" I said angrily.

I pointed across the room. "That's my husband and that's my children." Then, I felt my body with my hands. "What is this?" This was my first interaction with the real me. The me that had been living inside that physical body. I could talk to the devil, but my family could not hear me. It was as though an invisible curtain kept the sound of our conversation from entering their realm.

Suddenly, another spirit came into the room. I heard a loud swishing sound and the devil was gone. Looking back, I believe that my mother had been praying for me right at that moment. It was the time she would normally be praying her nightly prayers. Satan thought he had me, but God sent this other angel to intervene because my mother's prayers intercepted what was going on right at that moment.

Your tears are bottled up in heaven, and my mom was a saint. God promises you your children if you live right.

This other spirit was bright, and it had a blueish glow. That spirit picked me up and within a flat second, I'm in heaven.

He laid me face down. I didn't get to see beautiful heaven like other stories I'd heard. I was face down and very cold.

Then I heard a BIG, booming voice and I knew it was God. I was SO scared! It is scary to be in the presence of God when you're not ready.

In His loud, thunderous voice, I heard Him ask "How well do you know my Son?"

I was so scared. I didn't dare look up for fear I would be consumed. What I could see of this space that I was in, with my face looking down to the cold ground that my naked body lay upon, didn't "look" like heaven. It was a dark, brownish place that seemed like it wasn't even heaven at all. I can only describe it as an in between place. It felt like a judgement room.

I was totally still. Paralyzed by fear, the only thing I could seem to move were my eyes as they opened wide with surprise. Thirty-seven years of memories flooded my mind. I remembered all those years with the Bible laying on the coffee table.

The Holy Spirit would remind me, "You need to read that." And I'd find excuses.

"I've got six kids."

"I gotta cook."

"I gotta take care of the baby."

I always had excuses – for thirty-seven years.

"How well do you know the Word?" God's thundering voice asked again.

I knew He was asking me how well I knew Jesus, the Word of God, even though I'd never heard it preached that Jesus was the Word of God.

The Bible says that, "it is appointed unto men once to die, but after this the judgment..." (Hebrews 9:27).

Suddenly, a calming presence came into the room. I knew it was Jesus. From my position lying face down on the floor, I lifted my head to look up. I was shocked to see that it wasn't the man I'd been told about. Instead, I saw the actual Word of God.

Up until that moment, I thought that if I went to church on Sundays and Wednesday nights, I could trust the preacher with what he taught me. But you can't.

God asked me, "How could you trust your eternal salvation to a man?"

Why would anyone trust their salvation on somebody else's word? If you know the Word, then you know that Philippians 2:12 says, ". . . work out your own salvation with fear and trembling."

You can confess your sins all you want to, but if you don't know the Word of God, you don't know Jesus. You know about Jesus, because somebody told you about Him. But you don't know the real Jesus until you know the truth, because He is the truth and life. You don't know truth and life until you put Him inside of you.

I looked up to see the Word of God towering over me. He was HUGE and the color of granite. The WORD . . . just awesome!

I realized instantly that I knew of Jesus, but I didn't KNOW Jesus. I knew about Jesus because of what I'd heard preached. But I never experienced and put Jesus, the Word, inside of me. I'd grown up in church, but never read the Bible. I didn't think I had to. Jesus is the Word of God and when He comes back it is going to be written on Him "the Word of God" (see Revelation 19:13).

Now . . .

I believe that you have to put the Word of God in you.

I believe that it has to be downloaded into your mind.

I believe that if you love Jesus, the Word of God, you want to know Him. You want to get into the word and write it on your heart.

The Bible separates the holy from the unholy. And when it goes into your brain, it separates all the trash you've ever read and all the stuff you've ever seen . . . all the stuff you've ever heard, and it perfects you from your head to your feet. I really believe that's why, at 82, I'm in such good health. From the day I was born again, to this very day, I never stopped putting the Word of God inside of me. But I'm getting ahead of the story.

I was guilty and I knew it. I did not know the Word of God. I had done nothing to get to know Him. I knew that if only I could have a second chance, I needed to read and really learn my Bible. And, as I heard the Father ask if I knew His Son, I hung my head in sadness and shame and shook my head no.

Immediately, I started descending, face first. It felt as though I was falling out of the sky. Quickly I descended into the darkest darkness I had ever seen. There is no darkness like the darkness you experience when cut off from God. Nobody is going with you. This is one trip you are going on your own. Words can't describe just how scary it is. It is incredibly lonely. It is SO awful!

Demonic spirits began to surround me. They came from every direction. The closer I got to the pit of darkness the more of them there were. My descent came to a stop as I hovered over hell. The smell of sulfur and rotting flesh filled the air. Several demons grabbed hold of my arms and legs and tried to wrap them with these disgusting, black ties which looked like seaweed covered in oil. I kicked and screamed, desperately trying to escape their clutches. They bound my feet together and then bound my hands in front of my chest so they could pull me into hell.

I could see what looked like hot lava bubbling beneath me. Fire was shooting up, and the screams . . . the screams of the people in hell are so loud and so painful to hear. Their bodies had what looked like burning flesh hanging off them. Then the bubbling lava and fire would go down a little bit until suddenly it shoots up again.

I saw souls of teenagers by the thousands. Satan is bringing in the souls of teenagers by the thousands and the Church is asleep! The devil is taking our children while we play church.

As the demons pulled me closer to hell, I remembered my Sunday school teacher when I was a little girl. That happy memory came bursting back in my mind. She pulled me up on her lap and braided my hair and put pretty little bows in it to match my little dress.

She said to me, "Betty, because I love you, I'm gonna teach you this song."

And in my mind, I could hear her sweetly singing, "Jesus loves me, this I know, for the Bible tells me so."

And, on my way to hell, as this little song that she taught me rang in my memory, I said, "Yes! Jesus loves me." I wept. "If I could just reach Jesus . . ."

I cried out to Jesus, "Please forgive me! Please, don't let me go to this awful place!"

As I cried out to Jesus, I was suddenly turned up right. In this vast darkness surrounding me, the sounds of hell screaming up beneath me, all I could see was one tiny star up in the heavens.

I looked at this one and only light and said to myself, "Oh, I gotta keep my eyes on that. I can't look down. I remember my preacher telling me about Peter. Peter looked down. I can't look down. It ain't water under me. It is hell!"

I kept my eye on that light and it began to get closer and closer. When that light got to me, I could see it was Jesus. And my spirit body got sucked up inside of His, and He burned out all the darkness that was in me. All the perverseness that I'd seen, all the lying, the drinking, the desire for fame, everything that was in me that was not of Him, He burned it totally out of me. I was set free, delivered! Then, He put me back into my earthly body.

Hospital reports say that I grabbed hold of the doctor, screaming, "Don't let me go back to hell! Don't let me go back to hell!" I pulled so hard on his coat that the buttons popped off.

"Please, help me!" I screamed. "Don't let me go back there. It's so cold and awful. It's so black and lonely!"

As I stabilized, I began to grow warm. I could feel the peace of God flowing over me.

Jesus appeared to me.

"Betty, I'll let you live if you'll go tell the whole world that I'm coming."

"Oh Jesus," I answered, "who do you think is going to believe a stripper?"

"Mary was a prostitute and she was in my ministry," he answered.

"But Lord, my husband left me." I was referring to Larry. I was raised up to believe that for someone like me to be right with God you had to go back with your first husband. "He's married. They've got kids. I can't get him back."

"The woman at the well had more husbands than you and she went and told many."

I knew that many people came into relationship with Jesus because of her testimony. I was running out of excuses.

"Well, Lord, I'm not educated. I'm not smart. I don't know how to read some of those words. I can't read a chapter of the Bible without missing words. How can I teach your Word?"

"Betty," Jesus said, "I'm going to give you the greatest professor in the whole world. He's going to teach you the Word of God."

"What's his name?" I asked.

"The Holy Spirit."

11

The Greatest Professor

For days, I felt as though I were floating. It was so peaceful. During this time of peace and rest, I did a lot of serious thinking. God had given me a second chance. I was reborn that Thanksgiving Day and now my life would need to reflect that change.

As soon as I arrived home, I got my Bible out. I opened it and got down on my knees.

"Holy Spirit!" I called out, "You better get in here and help me or I'm going to tell Jesus on you!"

Looking back, I know how crazy that sounds. I came out of a world of sin. I was used to running my mouth and I didn't know how to talk to anyone yet, let alone the Holy Spirit. But the Holy Spirit was gentle. He didn't come at me with anger. He was so sweet, as though I'd never talked to Him like that.

He got right down on the ground beside me and softly said to me, "Honey, go get your tape recorder and a copy of the Bible on tape and let's play it and read it at the same time."

So, I did just that.

Every time I'd miss a word, He'd say, "Go back. Let's do this one again." I'd rewind the tape and read it again and again until I learned how to pronounce and say that word. For seven years, I did this every – single – day.

In the car, I played it. When I went to bed at night, I played it.

Holy Spirit said, "Betty, if you'll play it all night, your memory is open while the other parts of your brain rest. All night long you are downloading that in your memory. You know, when people were cruel to you, when they hurt you, and all these things up here in your head that you think about? As the Word goes in, it's going to delete them. My Word is a consuming fire and it's going to burn up everything in your brain that is contrary to my Word.

I thought, "Boy, this is GOOD."

So, I started playing that Bible every single night – all night long.

In the theaters that I danced in, there were often sex movies (pornography) playing in the theater. I wasn't into that, and I never watched them. But I could hear them playing as I was getting ready in my dressing room behind the screen. Three times a night for the better part of ten years those sounds found a home in my brain. Now God's Word would go in and burn every one of them out of my mind forever.

My husband, George, personally witnessed everything I went through as I left my body. And he watched once again as I came back into it, screaming and pulling on the doctor's coat as I begged him, "Don't let me die! I don't want to go back to hell!"

My anxiety didn't end when I went home from the hospital. In fact, it got so bad some days that George and Judy would have to put me out. If we were watching something on television and a nurse would give a shot or anything that would bring that memory back, it would immediately trigger me. I would begin shaking all over and I would start hyperventilating. I refused to take nerve pills. I didn't want anything controlling me. I was afraid I'd get hooked on those drugs. I was afraid of everything. Most importantly, I was afraid that any kind of medicine might usher me back to hell in an instant. So, George would have to hold me down on the floor and force me to take a nerve pill just to get me calmed back down again.

"You're alright, Betty. You're not dying. It'll be okay," George assured me. "Everything is going to be okay,"

The plan was to keep me sedated until I got better from this irrational behavior I was experiencing.

You can't imagine something as horrible as hell. Just try to imagine it. People are screaming violently. You're surrounded by fire and their flesh is falling off of them with every flash of the flames rising higher. And you know that you are about to go in that place with them!

Inside, I was convinced that if I said the wrong thing, at any moment, I might be right back in that fiery furnace of hell. Before this experience, I had a heck of a mouth on me. Being in the kind of environment I'd been in for so many years, I'd picked up quite the knack for cussing and other such useless language. Now, I was so scared that I would be struck dead if I spoke even one wrong word.

I used to be really bad at getting frustrated with other drivers. If someone pulled out in front of me, or did something wrong on the road, I'd start cussing those people out.

"Go to hell!" I'd yell out my car window.

But after my trip there, I learned to control that part of me really well.

I was out one day riding with Judy when someone cut in front of me.

"I hope you go to . . ." I screamed. But before that last word came out of my mouth, my brain realized what was about to happen. My eyes squinted and my body twitched, ". . .heaven!"

Judy said, "That was good, Mama."

That entire experience had such a dramatic effect on my life. I will never be the same. For forty years after, I never went to a hospital. I didn't even go to a doctor for the next ten years. But that is just how scared I was of ever having a chance of reliving that again.

After my experience, I remember so vividly the peace and love I felt when I saw Jesus, and also the torment and pain I felt when I saw hell. I wanted everyone I met to be able to see Jesus and I wanted to save everyone I could from ever going to hell. I had a desperation to do it. I had a drive like you've never seen. You can't believe the number of people I've won to Jesus all these years. And I've never yet had anyone tell me no.

I would even get on the city bus and win somebody to Jesus and say to the bus driver, "I'll pay you to let me ride this bus and win people to Jesus. I'll pay for everyone who rides too." I was willing to pay them big money. My husband had it. I didn't care. I'd pay to preach.

I would stop my car in the middle of the main road on Miami Beach and stop traffic while I got on top of my car to preach. I'd walk into a club, stop everything and climb up on the stage and give my testimony.

I was in the newspaper almost every week. The news media would come out and cover me, trying to make me look bad. The headline would read:

Ex-stripper Preaching on the Street

Whenever reporters would try to make me look bad, at that moment, they would fall over onto the ground and get saved. Every reporter did.

It wasn't long before word got out about "the former stripper who became a street preacher".

A Lutheran church, nearby, asked me to come to give my testimony. The church used a photo of me from my show business days in their advertisement and people came from EVERYWHERE.

Before I went to speak there, the Holy Spirit said to me, "Open your mouth and I will fill it."

I wasn't sure what to expect. Part of me was excited at the chance to save people from an eternity in hell, but another part of me was very nervous.

When the people quit singing, I walked up to the pulpit to speak. I was sure I was about to burst into tears. I remembered what the Lord had said to me before and whispered inside my mind, "God, if you don't give me something, I'm going to sit down!" I thought. Then, I heard His gentle whisper, "Pray."

I opened my mouth to pray and it was like turning a key to a car. It kept running and running. I thought I would never stop. By the time I was finished, the people were all crowded around the alter, tears in their eyes. "Please, help me. I am a pimp. Help me change."

"I am a bartender," another called out.

There were people from the clubs, bartenders, and pimps. I was thinking, "Man, this church is filled with sinners."

Close to two hundred people got saved and delivered that day.

After the meeting, the pastor called me to his office.

He said, "Betty, where did you get all these people?"

"I don't know them," I said with surprise. "I thought they were your church."

More and more newspaper articles came out and more and more I saw the body of Christ being healed. Not just physical healing. Churches began to pack out. Pastors from different denominations would have services together.

I saw a Church of God pastor and an Assembly of God pastor, who were previously not talking to each other, now casting out devils together.

It seemed as though all the Christian groups in our town had been delivered of the spirit of jealousy.

More and more I told my story and more and more I saw people delivered from all kinds of sicknesses and spirits.

Next, the 700 Club heard of me and asked if they could come to Miami to film my story.

We were at one of the clubs and I was putting on makeup before we began filming. The interviewer and I began to pray in tongues. When the cameraman arrived, I suddenly realized...

Here I was, sitting in my own dressing room where I once was the star for Satan, praying in tongues. Now, this same room would be used to tape my story and set people free!

For many years that followed, I would tell my story again and again. I can't even recall how many times my story has been told. I haven't begun to count the number of television shows I've appeared on. I've even appeared on secular shows like The Joan Rivers Show, Maury Povich, and Sally Jesse Raphael.

Before long, Morris Cerullo came to Miami and offered a Bible school.

There was a very wealthy lady who decided that she was going to go to his school. She later shared this story with me:

She had paid her tuition and that night God kept her awake all night long.

"It's not your turn," the Lord spoke to her. "I want you to wait. I have a girl and I want you to give your tuition money to her." Then, He brought my face before her.

The next day, she went to a place called Pass It On. It was a place that gave food out to the needy. That same day, God sent me to hand out Bibles to everyone that I won to Jesus, and I won 'em all. So, I bought cases and cases of Bibles and I'd give one to every person.

A lot of people came to Pass it On. All day long. God had assigned me to win every person to Him that would come for food. And I did.

I would fast every day until 2:00 p.m.

Because I'd seen so many people in hell, I could not even eat breakfast until I'd go out and win somebody to Jesus. I had to keep them out of that horrible place.

"Oh my God, I've got to keep people from going to hell," I'd fret constantly.

"I can't stand it. I can't live like this," I cried. "I've got to stop people from going there." I'd go out in the streets, to bus stops, everywhere and anywhere. And I'd win people to Jesus.

I guess it was because I had such a hunger inside of me, and such compassion for others. I was still playing the Bible on tape every night, too. The anointing on me was so strong that even when they didn't speak English, I would go into tongues and win them all around the room.

This young man walked in at Pass it On. He had dropped his wife off earlier to get food. I done won everybody in the room, and when he walked in, I put my hands out and said to him, "Jesus said that you are ready to receive Him right now, aren't you?" Tears streamed down from his eyes and he walked across the room and received Jesus. You never seen anything like it.

So, when Morris came to town, this wealthy woman (everyone at Pass It On called her Granny) told 'em what God had told her about the lady in her vision. They said, "I know who that is... Betty Green."

That night she called me, "You don't know me. My name is Shirley. God told me to pay your way to Morris Cerullo's Bible College. I've already paid. All you've got to do is show up."

Well, God told me not to read no man's books and He told me I could only have virgin word of the Bible.

"I only want you to read My book," is what He said to me. So, I said, "I am not interested in no man but the Word of God." Then I hung up on her.

I was listening to God. I'd been to hell. Ain't nobody gonna steer me wrong.

I called and talked to my pastor's wife and she started praying in the spirit. I had never heard her talk in tongues. And that scared me. I thought, "I better listen to her."

That Sunday, my pastor said, "Betty, I'd rather you go to his school than anybody in my church," (and it was a big church). "I know you have a call on your life."

So, he took me and a bunch of others from my church to Morris' school. When I first started, it was like I kept expecting our pastor to pick us up and take us out of there any minute because Morris was coming against everything I'd ever been taught – all traditions, religion, and judgmental spirits, etc.

It was like I was sitting there, and he was pulling all this stuff out of my mouth. Just pulling and pulling. And when he got through, it's like he threw bleach in my mouth and it was bleaching me all the way down to my toes.

I walked over to my pastor and I said, "Pastor, why didn't you tell us this stuff?" He looked at his wife and said, "I knew she'd get it."

That school changed me. I was very judgmental at this time in my life. But in this Bible school, I learned how to have compassion for others.

In the school, Morris asked us to write out our personal testimony and turn it in. I thought everybody had a life like I did! I didn't think nothing about it, and I turned it in. Then they came to see me. Morris wanted me to get up and tell the whole class my testimony about dying, going to hell ... how I got saved.

I had such an anointing on me that the people didn't want me to stop talking.

He had me in five years of Bible school – over and over and over again. During that time, Morris became my spiritual daddy. God really wanted me to get the Jewish aspect. Morris was a Jewish boy, you see. Learning the Bible from a Jewish perspective, as a baby Christian, really helped me. When a Messianic Jewish person teaches you the Bible it's different, more thorough, better. He was the most amazing teacher of my life. I never saw anything like it.

When he walked out on the stage, the power of God was so strong that, if you didn't change, you'd feel compelled to leave.

So, I really came out of that school so anointed. I started fasting and praying - big time. And about that time, Morris' staff called me "Morris Junior" because of the anointing.

Then, I began to go out all over the state and set up Bible schools for Morris.

After several years of Bible school, and all the opportunities to share my testimony, I began to travel and preach.

Lester Sumrall heard about me and he called and wanted me to be on his TV station. After I appeared with him there, he asked if he could book me in all his churches. He like me because I cast out devils.

One of those churches was in Rock Island, Illinois. 700 people were slain in the spirit during that service. As soon as I asked them to come forward, they all fell down.

I worked with Dr. Sumrall for several years, preaching in his churches. Many, many miracles happened in each of those services.

I remember a man in Milwaukee. His body was so twisted, and he couldn't walk or talk. I prayed over him and cast that devil out of him. He got out of that chair and was dancing!! Praise be to God!

Back in Miami, after another amazing service where all kinds of strippers, drug addicts, and others were delivered and healed, I got a call the next morning from two gentlemen. "God told me to give you money to go to the Philippines," one of them said.

They came over and gave me $3,000!!

So, I prepared a group of women from my Bible school to go on a crusade with me to the Philippines.

My husband told me that if I would call a travel agent that they would set me up.

"I'd like to go with you," George said, "because when I was in the service, I was stationed over there. So, just call the travel agent and tell them that you've got three thousand dollars and they'll set it all up for you."

I picked up the phone and dialed.

A man answered the phone.

"Hello, my name is Betty Green. I'd like to set up travel arrangements to take a group of Bible students on a trip to hold a crusade in the Philippines."

The man on the other end of the line said, "You've got the wrong number, but it's the right number. This is God. . . . uh, don't hang up!"

"I called a travel agent and you tell me you're God?" I asked with a tone of skepticism bordering on rudeness. "Who is this?" I asked.

He said, "I'm the president of Korean airlines. God just spoke to me and told me that it is not to the

Philippines that He is trying to send you, but you have a mandate in South Korea at Dr. Cho's."

He said, "I believe this is God so strongly, here's what I'm going to do for you. I'm going to set you up in an American hotel near Dr. Cho's, where you're safe. You're going to go to Dr. Cho's on Thursday night for all night prayer. You're going to go on Sunday to Prayer Mountain." He listed out all the things I would do in South Korea and told me all about the worldwide revival they were having.

"A million people are going to be there and be saved," he said. "Then, I'm going to send you on to the Philippines to do your crusade. You're going to be tired after that, so I'm going to send you for a 3-day weekend in China so you can rest up before you fly back to the United States. All for $1,500 each."

That was almost a month of the fanciest hotels you could stay in, food . . . everything. I was headed to South Korea!

12

Building Mountains

Before going to South Korea, I gathered all of the women who were going with me and we prayed. We saw demonic spirits come down. We really did our job before we ever went there. We didn't have nothing coming against us, because we had done our spiritual warfare ahead of time.

At that time, Russia was talking about bombing America. I was trying to find out how we could keep Russia from blowing us up.

When I got to South Korea, Dr. Yonggi Cho was having a big convention with all kinds of preachers from all over the globe. When I saw the line of preachers waiting to talk with him, I thought, "He's never going to see me, he's got all these big shots here." Then Lydia Swain, his assistant, came over and said, "Betty Green, Dr. Cho will see you first." I thought I'd pass out!

"You speak English so well! Are you American too?" I asked.

"Yes, I am," she smiled. "When you come back again, I want you to bring me some perfume. I just can't find what I like here."

I go in, with my women, to see Dr. Cho and I'm afraid to talk because some preachers don't like when women speak up. We lived in a time when woman preachers weren't accepted by most. I didn't want to be outspoken. I wanted him to start the conversation.

Ultimately, I'm not the kind of person to beat around the bush, so I said, "Dr. Yonggi Cho, I want to know how you like women preachers?"

He grinned. "Well, I have 500." He said, "You know, I would really like you to minister in my crusade. I would've made you my number one speaker, but I've already asked Billy Graham." I didn't know that Dr. Cho even knew anything about me!

Now, if I had spoken at this event I would've become very famous. It was that big of a deal. I quickly remembered when I was between heaven and hell and I promised, "I'll never give no man the glory, but You."

A stripper's greatest dream is to see her name in neon lights and be famous. And this invitation to speak at Dr. Cho's crusade, all of the sudden, was like Vegas. And I saw that feeling rising in me and so I told Dr. Cho, "No."

I quickly humbled myself, before the Lord struck me dead.

"I didn't come here to speak or preach," I said. "I came here to pray for America and seek God. Can I go to your Prayer Mountain?"

He sent me on a bus with my group to Prayer Mountain. We arrived at the welcome center in short order. As I walked in, I noticed a large marble carving of the Bible. It looked just like that same vision of Jesus that I'd had when I was hanging between this world and the next, that same Bible I'd seen in heaven! I thought, "Boy, somebody had to have a vision of heaven to be able to make that identical to what I had seen." That scared me. I knew I was on holy ground when I saw that.

A guide took us on a tour and showed us around.

All over the side of the mountain are these little, shed-like dorms, called prayer cells. Inside each one, there's a rug on the floor and a cross. You just go in there and lay down on that carpet in front of that cross and pray.

There's no room for two people, just one. So, we go in and pray. We had been praying for about an hour when somebody knocks on my door.

I opened my door to see a guard standing there with a gun. Now, I'm in a foreign country and I know I'm in a war zone on the border of North Korea. So, I thought to myself, "I better do what he says."

"Come with me. Hallelujah Mama wants to see you."

I didn't even know she existed. I didn't know anything about her. At that time, Mama Choi was more famous in South Korea than Dr. Cho. She was his mother-in-law and the one who founded the Prayer Mountain, then she took a back seat and pushed him out in front. She did all the work, fasting and praying then, when people got saved, she would send them to his church.

I also did not know that she had visited America at the request of President Reagan.

After the attempted assassination of President Reagan, I'm told he asked, "Has any nation ever been turned around through prayer?"

Mama Choi would later tell me about the president telling her of his supernatural encounter with God after he was shot in the failed attempt against him.

That's when he heard of the powerful success of Prayer Mountain in South Korea, so he invited Dr. Choi, along with two other well-known Christian leaders in America, to have a special meeting with him at the White House. At this meeting, she promised to help him turn the nation back to God through prayer and to get prayer back in America's schools.

On the way back to South Korea, she got on the wrong plane because she couldn't read English.

And when she got home, Dr. Cho told her, "Mama, that cost you money to get another plane ticket. If you are going to continue to travel to America, you need a companion to travel with you. Go to Prayer Mountain and get some women to pray with you. Ask God to send you an American woman that will work with you so that you can do what President Reagan has asked you to do."

So, she got 60,000 women to pray for God to send an American woman to help her.

The guard took me to Mama (Ja-Shil) Choi's house. As I walked in, she came through the beads hanging in the doorway.

Later, she would tell me, "When I came through the beads and saw Betty Green, God spoke to me and said, 'This is the woman you've been praying for. I sent her.' It was like my own daughter had come home."

She had lost her daughter, and by that point in my life, I had lost my mom. And it was like my mom walked in and her daughter walked in, and God united us and knit our hearts – mother and daughter right there in that place, in that moment. It was supernatural.

Of all the women all over the world God could send, why in the world would he send somebody as ignorant as me? Because she prayed, "God send me somebody compatible to me." She wanted somebody to love her, take care of her, and look after her, and I did.

I saw how they prayed, and I said, "This is what we need in America."

You have no idea how hard they prayed. They cried with tears running down their face. They were sincere. You don't see that much in America.

When I got home, I was approached by a small group of people who were leaving Morris Cerullo. They wanted to launch me out into television ministry and to begin doing crusades of my own. I said, "I'm concerned that we might be doing something that Morris doesn't approve of." And I loved him so much. He's my spiritual daddy. There's no way I'm going to do anything without him doing it with me or putting his blessing on it.

I told them, "I can't take you away from him."

"We're leaving him anyway," they replied.

"You give me thirty days to fast and pray," I responded.

A few days later, I was at home when I heard a knock on my door. There was a man and a woman standing there. I had never seen them before in my life.

He introduced himself as Jim Goff, then he introduced his wife, and though he'd never known me or seen me before, he seemed confident in his message. "God sent me," he said.

I invited the two of them into my home. "Please, have a seat on the couch."

"Betty, God said that he is getting ready to bring together the two biggest anointings from two different countries to take the nation for Him. You are wanting to take Miami. It's just one city, and He is trying to give you the world." He continued to prophesy to me.

I don't even know how he got in my building. You had to have a security card to get in. But I knew in my spirit that this message was indeed from God.

I hadn't even gotten through the thirty days of fasting and prayer, and here was my answer. These were amazing years and I loved every minute of working with Morris Cerullo. But it was time to move on to God's new season for me.

I wrote to Mama Choi and I asked her, "Would you come to America? Would you help me start a Prayer Mountain here?"

"Yes, I will," she answered. And so, she went to Lydia Swain and told her to write me that she was coming. Lydia told me that I would be responsible for her in the United States. So, Mama Choi came to the United States. I met up with her in California at LAX.

It was an awesome season in my life. I travelled with Mama (Dr. Ja-Shil) Choi for many years. Often, two or three assemblies would come together and set up a big crusade for us. There were four of us who travelled together: me, Mama Choi, her doctor and her nurse.

Once, Dr. Choi and I were holding a crusade in Texas. There were over 1,500 people there. First, she preached. As she did, I noticed a young man who was deaf. I could tell because I could see that he was doing sign language.

I was so upset because she did not pray for him. But, when she was finished, she handed me the mic and asked me to take the offering. So, I prayed, and we took up the offering. Then, I called that young man up for prayer.

He was 17 years old. I stuck my fingers in his ears and commanded, "You deaf and dumb spirit, I bind you. Come out of him!"

I stepped back and held my hand in front of my mouth. I didn't want him to see what I was saying. Then, I said, "Say Jesus."

He said, "Je-sus." His eyes widened in surprise. Then he began to scream over and over again. "Jesus! Jesus!"

Dr. Choi came up out of her chair and ran down to me. She was praising God all the way. The entire place jumped to their feet and praised the Lord.

Hundreds of people were healed that night. The whole time, I had no idea that $40,000 had been given in the offering that evening. The Holy Spirit took up that offering, not me.

You see, I learned to depend on the Holy Spirit. I just let Him use my body to do what He pleased.

After that awesome meeting, Dr. Choi told her son, Pastor Mark S. Kim, that I was a prophet and that he should get me to the homes of all the businessmen who supported their church so I could pray for them and bless them.

Without my knowing what was going on, I was invited to hundreds of homes over the years. Each time, they would hand me checks for hundreds of dollars. I told Pastor Kim that I felt bad taking it. But he insisted I receive their gifts as they were sowing for their miracle to come to their business.

Mama Choi and I held crusades all over the United States and we never took from the offering. I earned all my money from selling my books. All the offerings that we received were collected together and used to start Full Gospel International Fasting Prayer Mountain in Romoland, California.

At first, this large piece of property in the mountains of California held only a trailer for Mama Choi to live in when she came to America. There was also an old building that had a kitchen in it. Then we brought in three more double wide trailers for the rest of us to stay in and to hold meetings. These held fifty people each.

Eventually, it grew and is now a larger facility with a dozen buildings on it, including men and women's dormitories, a thousand seat auditorium, and a chapel that seats five hundred. Each dormitory building houses a large classroom that can hold a hundred seats each. Generally, churches come and rent the buildings for their retreats.

During the building of this special place, I continued to live in Miami with my family. I would travel back and forth to California to hold crusades with Mama Choi and to help with Prayer Mountain, often staying months at a time. I also travelled to every television station in the United States that would have me so I could promote Prayer Mountain.

Then, in 1989, during a visit to this Prayer Mountain that we had founded together, Mama Choi asked me to meet with her. We had been traveling and preaching together every summer for many years by this point.

Mama Choi said, "Betty, if you are going to work with me you are going to have to fast with me." She put me in a room where I was the only one who spoke English. I was there for three days. I started to think, "She changed my plane ticket. She brought me here. Nobody speaks English".

I had been on the road preaching for three months. I was so tired and burned out and I had no one to speak to in English.

The devil started to whisper in my ear, "They've kidnapped you. You are never going home."

Every thought that you could imagine came in my mind. After a while, I got serious with God. I started praying and seeking God's face and I started getting rid of self and I spent those three days with God seriously strong. After the third day, Mama Choi sent for me.

When I entered her room, she was sitting on the edge of her bed.

"Betty, sit here in front of me," she said.

She had me sit down on the floor in front of her, between her legs, with my back to her.

Her son, Pastor Kim, was in the room with us. He had come to town from the LA Korean church, where he was pastor. He said, "Betty, Mama sent for me because she has broken English and she wants to be sure that you are going to really understand what she is about to say to you."

"OK," I said.

"My mother is getting too old to travel like she has been doing. God has spoken to her and told her that she is to lay her mantle on you."

I had no idea what a mantle was.

Her son said, "What she wants you to understand is that she is going to pray over you and lay her mantle on you today."

She placed her hands on my shoulders and began to pray. Then she put them on my head and released her mantle on me right there in that little trailer on Prayer Mountain.

She said, "Daughter, we need to go back to Washington D.C. I have a covenant with them. You have to go with me so you can have the covenant to carry it on and finish it."

She wanted to go back to the White House to do it so she could tell President Reagan that she was keeping her covenant with him and that she was laying her mantle on me, and now I was in charge of seeing this through. Mama Choi believed in covenants – big time. I do too.

A special event was set up at the White House and we prepared ourselves to attend. But she was having some challenges with her health. She had been in the hospital just prior to this trip to the U.S., but I didn't know it. That was one of the reasons that she wanted me to take over.

We both flew into Washington, D.C., separately and met up together there. We stayed with the Korean pastoral pastor who oversaw all the Korean pastors throughout Washington, D.C. and Virginia.

Eventually, that special day came, and a ceremony took place at the White House where the official passing of responsibility from Mama Choi to me occurred. The room was packed with prayer coordinators from near and far. There were several hundred people in attendance, including representatives from the 700 Club.

I spoke first and introduced her to the gathering of people. As I did, I could feel the cold stares from many in the room.

First off, we were the only two women I even remember being there. The place was packed out with men in church leadership. I could tell by the way they looked at me that they were wondering how such a wise, educated, spiritual leader such as Dr. Ja-Shil Choi could choose a country girl like me to be her successor.

I called her Mama Choi instead of Dr. Choi. That made a few eyes widen at my blunder. The men in the room applauded and stood as Mama Choi came to the front of the room. She put her arms around me and hugged me and kissed me. Then she turned to address those who had gathered for the occasion.

"This is my USA daughter," Mama Choi said. "I LOVE Betty Green."

I think there were many in the room who were expecting intellectual stuff, but they got love instead. And they couldn't handle it. Everyone was surprised that Dr. Choi chose me. But she didn't choose me, God did.

The man who was the announcer that day, clearly did not approve. Something in the atmosphere with all these strong, accomplished men, and me this little country girl who did not deserve to be there, made me feel like I was simply nothing standing there.

Suddenly, another gentleman stood and began to prophesy, and with a loud voice he proclaimed, "I, God, chose Betty Green. It was I!"

It was so strong that men all over the room began to hit the floor. I stood there with tears streaming down my face. I was so happy that God would stick up for little ol' me. To know that God loved me and would make known that He had chosen me, even before all of these influential people, it is one of the most precious memories of my life. God is so good to me. I don't even understand it.

That day, Mama Choi made it official to everyone else that she was handing her "mantle" – her responsibility – to help bring America back to the Lord and prayer back to our schools, on to me.

Later that evening she flew back to California. I was headed back to Texas, or I would've travelled to California with her. Her job was now over but mine was beginning. I had to go to work. In Dallas, I had a big meeting which I had left to go to Washington, and I needed to get back and finish it.

I got to my hotel that night, showered, and got in bed, then the phone rang. I got out of bed and reached for the phone, and when I did, I felt this weighted sensation on my shoulders. It was so heavy it put me down on my knees. When I picked up the phone, Helen Ko, Director of Prayer Mountain in California., was on the other end of the line.

She said, "Mama . . ."

"She just passed away, didn't she?" I asked.

"How do you know?"

"The mantle just transferred to my shoulders. And it put me to the floor."

Helen and I wept together.

I flew back out to Prayer Mountain the next day. Once there, I took Helen to the airport so she could fly back to South Korea for the funeral.

Pastor Kim ran up to me when he saw me at the airport. He hugged me so tightly and cried like a baby. "Please go with us," he begged, "I'll pay your way."

But I insisted on staying behind to take care of things at Prayer Mountain while everyone else flew home for Mama Choi's funeral. At the time, I thought it was the most helpful thing I could do. And my pride kept me from accepting his generous offer. I wish someone had talked me out of it. Missing her funeral is the single greatest mistake I ever made in my life.

In South Korea, everybody wanted to know where I was. Where was this "daughter" who couldn't attend her "mother's" funeral? I should've been there. But there are no do-overs in life. Most of the time, we get only one chance to make right choices. Fortunately, for me, I was given a second chance from God when it counted most.

I continued to visit and minister at Prayer Mountain for years after Mama Choi went home to the Lord.

During one such visit, I was teaching at three different services. The last one was all businessmen.

Pastor Kim asked, "Pastor Betty, do you remember all those homes I took you to and you blessed them?

"Yes," I answered.

"Today they are all millionaires."

God never ceases to amaze me.

The following year, Morris Cerullo was launching his new network and he decided that I had advanced and he wanted me to be the first one to go on television to represent the school of ministry with him.

I was dressed and made up, waiting in the wings. I was ready to walk up on stage to do it. And God said, "Do you remember when you hung between heaven and hell? And you promised you'd never give no man the glory but me?"

I turned around, tears streaming down my face, "I can't do it." I said to the stage manager.

A puzzled look took over her face. "Why?" She asked.

You see, in the past, I wanted fame so badly it took me to hell. I worked hard for years in show business to show the world that I was somebody!

Eventually, I learned how to live a fasted life to keep that ugly spirit from rising back up in me.

All of this occurred to me as I made my way to the stage and, suddenly, I realized that I needed to humble myself. I never wanted to disappoint God again and I certainly didn't want to go back to hell.

"I promised God I would never give anybody glory but Him, as I hovered over hell."

She held me by my shoulders, "Betty, Brother Cerullo will understand that."

And I walked away.

I had absolutely no idea what God had in store for me next. I only knew that it was going to be awesome. And it was.

13

Moving Mountains

I've had an exciting life. I've done a ton of stuff. My favorite, by far, is serving the Lord.

When I was a little girl, about five or six years old, my mother taught me an important lesson.

We were out walking in the woods, and she bent over to pick up a rock covered in green moss. "Do you see this rock?" she asked me.

"Yes, Mama."

"This moss is like mold, and it's no good. It deteriorates it. A rolling stone never catches moss."

That always stuck in my mind. Satanic things, and the devil, and sin was moss. It intimidated me. As I encountered sin over the course of my life, I kept rolling. Every time I got knocked down or got sick, I jumped back up and kept moving. I won't take it!

I am the temple of the Holy Ghost. "You're not attaching yourself to me. You are my enemy! Disease, sickness, loneliness, despair you are not in me. I love Jesus. I belong to Him and I'm not whore hopping."

I knew how much it hurt my mama for my daddy to fool around with other women. Each time he gave a little piece of himself away, a piece of my mama's heart died with it. I will not do that to Jesus.

I've always felt that way about sin. For a while, I lived with resentment and bitterness. My daddy gave me away to a husband that didn't love me. My husband gave up on me and left me for a younger woman. No one cared about me. My church even rejected me because my husband left me. And that made me turn bitter.

Everywhere I turned, love escaped me, and it made me grow cold. It made me build walls around my heart. It made me not care about myself either. People were not for me and I thought God didn't love me, neither. So, I turned to a life of sin.

But even while I was off for a little while, I still had some faith in me. And this new lifestyle of mine made me understand sin and brokenness more than I ever had. No wonder we could not minister to some of the men in our congregation. We really did not understand what they were battling.

Through that time spent as a stripper, I learned a lot about people. I learned about hurt and problems. I learned how we hurt each other. I learned about why we hurt and how we should listen to each other. I wrote a book about marriage just from what I heard from men talking to me in the club about their hurts.

I would talk to these young girls who would come in to dance and I'd discourage them from the lifestyle and try to look after and protect them. I wasn't in the clubs fornicating like some of the others. I was there to make a living. Just like that rock moving and not gathering moss, I was going to be there and move and accomplish my purpose of making a living and that club wasn't going to get on me.

"I'm rolling out of here," I'd say.

I saw others get consumed with liquor and drugs. I didn't want nothing controlling me that I couldn't turn loose. And I made up my mind that no man is going to have sex with me unless it's MY decision. That was my attitude.

"If I'm going to sin, it's going to be my choice. I'm not going to get in bondage to it." And none of that stuff did take me over.

But I did catch "moss". While sex, and drugs, and drinking did not get their ugly claws in me, the desire for fame most certainly did. And that desire for fame and beauty nearly cost me my life. It nearly cost me an eternity in hell.

When the devil told me that I was an unfit mother and that a real mother would dance for that money, I said, "I'll show you!"

All I ended up doing was showing myself. I showed myself that you can't win when you give in to enticement.

When you are exposed to so much ugliness, it makes your heart harder and harder. Especially when you see people that you know falling so far from purity.

No matter what you've been through, I've been through it. I understand. I think that all the things that's been done to me, helped me to understand people. And I can have compassion for people and help you to get delivered. Because I overcame it, you can overcome it, too.

Whatever may be fighting you in your body, in your mind, or in your spirit, God has a way out for you. Get in your Bible. Get to know the Word of God. Do like I did.

I played that Bible recording day after day. I downloaded that Bible into my brain. You are just going to get what you go and do. You got to go and do it if you want it! You got to know Jesus to preach Jesus. And when you get Him inside of you, He's loud. It's Him coming out of you. It ain't you no more. You are in the back and He is in the lead. He knows this stuff better than I do.

I learned a long time ago that the Holy Spirit is the greatest professor in the world. Why would I want to do it when I can turn Him loose and He makes me look good? Because He is good. So, I let him do everything. Then everybody thinks I'm smart (I am. I yield.).

Yield to the Holy Spirit and let Him speak to you, but you've got to get the Word in you. He said, "I'll bring it to your remembrance." But if you haven't put anything in you, there isn't anything for Him to help you remember. So, you've got to put it inside you. That's why you want to play that Bible and listen to it over and over.

Just going to church and listening to your preacher is not enough.

I see people sitting in churches week after week still living lukewarm lives. That grieves my spirit. How can people just live and never consecrate themselves unto God? We get so much out of that. And it keeps us walking in the Spirit. Don't you know that you've got to be like Him? Don't you know you've got to do what He's done? How on earth are you going to live in heaven living like you do? He's not going to put up with the stuff we're doing here.

I think I've lived too long. I think people want to retire me, because I'm too old thinking. But I can't comprehend how people can live that way when they can live like I'm living and enjoy it so much!

I feel that this time in my life is an adventure. I believe that God wants me to share my story and share the Word of God. I'd love to put one of my Bible schools in every city in the whole United States.

I have a holy fear of God, but when He promises me something, I trust Him. I know He's going to do it. And I have that kind of relationship with Him.

I was sitting next to Jesus one day in the grass. We were watching a hundred women at a meeting in Miami. The women were praising God and just weeping.

I said, "Jesus, isn't this precious? Isn't it sweet?"
"No."

"Jesus, you're not watching, look. Look how sweet. They're crying."

"No, it's sad."

"What do you mean? Why is it sad?" I asked.

"Betty, when they come in and they start worshiping Me, they come into My presence. It's My presence that makes them cry. But upon leaving My presence, they walk back out those doors, and take up their old habits and way of life. And only twenty of that one-hundred will make it."

This is how we talk all the time. And I have His presence all the time. I really believe it's because I sacrifice regularly. And I gave up my will. It was about two years after my trip to hell.

I wrote up a power of attorney document. I'd learned how to create those back in the days when I was selling cars with George. I had seen how self being in charge had so misdirected my life. I didn't trust me anymore. I signed that power of attorney.

"God, I saw myself on that bed," I prayed out loud. "I saw what self did to me. I can't trust it. I don't trust me no more. I'm not strong enough," I began to cry. "I don't want no will. I know you gave me a free will, but I don't want it no more."

I reached down, grabbed the power of attorney document and raised it up to the Lord. "Here," I said quietly. "I made this legal and binding, Lord. Take it. You give me yours and take mine." From that day, I only do what God wants me to do. As far as I'm concerned, I don't have a will.

If I'm not supposed to go somewhere, He'll block me. It won't happen. But if I'm supposed to go somewhere, the gates of hell can't stop it.

Will you give your will to God? Right now, cup your hands and hold them out in front of you. Why do you want your will anyway? Don't you want to be in God's will all the time? Wouldn't it be awesome to be walking in His perfect will and be blessed everywhere you turn?

So, put your will in your hands, right now. Think about how you are going to please Him. See Him smiling. He can use you for anything He wants to do because you submitted.

Now, throw it up to Him.
Here is my challenge to you: don't take it back. Now, if you really mean it, He takes it and He'll give you His will like he did me.

I don't desire mine because I'm too scared of it. I know what my will did to me.

BEFORE:
Viccki Lee
Satan's Angel, the Devil's Own Mistress

AFTER:
Reverend Betty Green
(Mama Choi on Left, Betty on Right)

There are a lot of lessons within the pages of my life story. You see where I was and how God turned it around. You've seen where He took me with that turnaround. No matter what you've done, you can turn your life around, too. There is hope in Jesus.

You've seen my before. . . a lonely mountain girl whose heart had been broken by men. A young lady who desperately wanted to be loved and respected. A woman who gave up on people and, in many ways, gave up on God and pursued a life in pursuit of fame and beauty instead.

I'm in awe of how my life has become a testimony to the salvation message.

God took my brokenness. He loved me so much that He literally saved me from the clutches of hell. And then He made me more beautiful than I could ever dream.

This is the kind of beauty that makeup and pretty dresses can't create. I'm talking about the kind of beauty that God finds most attractive. Does God appreciate physical beauty?

Well, let me ask you . . . have you seen a sunset on the beaches of California? The Grand Canyon? The twinkle in your child's eyes when they see you come home from a long day at work? If you've ever seen spring flowers covering the mountains of North Carolina, then you know that He does.

But beauty is not just about what we see. To God, beauty is more about the heart. It is about the things a person does. It's about who you are and whose you are – a child of the most high God.

If you'll let Him, He will deliver you from a life of sin and He will restore you to the life He always intended for you, just like He did with me.

Remember those tapes I played over and over as the Holy Spirit taught me the Word of God? I still play them while driving all over the USA to preach (though it's on CD now). For over 40 years I've played the Word of God to myself as faith comes by hearing. By hearing, I walk in faith. And you can do this too!

Remember my Aunt Susie Mae? Even though there had been a divide there for years, Mama and Aunt Susie Mae had long since made peace with each other. Aunt Susie Mae eventually went on to remarry and she had many more children.

Recently, through Facebook and family reunions, I was united with these cousins that I didn't even know I had. I am so excited to be a part of their life and they with mine. What the devil had meant for destruction of a family, God healed and brought restoration to it. He always aims to move us towards good.

The same was true for me and my mama. Not long after I was literally born again and saved from the grips of death, God restored my relationship with Mama. We became quite close. I'm so happy I had those few years to spend with her in that way before she went home to Jesus.

When she could no longer be with me, the Lord sent me Dr. Choi to be my "mama". They both taught me many things, especially how to become closer to God.

And now, I too have become a mama. I have six children that I adore. I wish I could spend more time with them. I love them SO much! And I have thousands of spiritual children, too. They call me "Mama Betty".

Like all mamas, I want more than anything to help my children and give them the best life possible. If I can give you just one thing to help you in this world, it would be to draw you closer to Jesus.

I realize that everyone has been through something tough in life. But I encourage you to turn your life completely over to Jesus.

And when the things of this world make life hard for you, do like my mama taught me – be like a rolling stone. Let no moss come upon you. Remind the devil, "You're not attaching yourself to me. You are my enemy!

Disease, sickness, loneliness, despair you are not in me. I love Jesus and I belong to Him!"

Yes, my mama was a very smart woman.

Afterword

The one thing I can tell you with full assurance, PRAYER MOVES MOUNTAINS (Mark 11:23-24).

My whole focus since my first trip to South Korea was to get prayer in schools and take America back for the Lord. I have a mandate to do that. And it will happen if I can get people to help me. I can't do it all by myself. Mama Choi had thousands of women to help her when she raised up Prayer Mountain in South Korea. I've got to have people who will work with me. Will you fast and pray for America with me?

In looking back over the story of my life and all that I've been through, the thing I have the deepest connection to is prayer and fasting—which is the extreme opposite to flesh.

Your flesh will take you to hell. And if you do not chasten it with fasting, prayer, and the Word of God, I doubt very seriously if you'll get into heaven.

People want to forget all that they know about God. They think that it's a new time and so we need to move on to something else. But I think that the Word of God is the Word of God – then, now and forever. God changes not.

Fasting is still good for today. It hasn't changed. In fact, He's not going to save America until we fast and pray.

I'm quite conscious of denying self. I deny myself all the time. I give to the point that I may not have coffee to drink. I may not have one dollar in my pocket. I just keep giving out. I give and give and give.

I do not say this to brag. I want no praises from men. I share it with you so that you can know how I really live. I can only share with you what I know.

I deny self all kinds of ways. Things I really want I give away. Then I say to myself, "Why'd I do that? I really liked that."

I discipline my "self" so it can never ever do what it did to me before.

But I don't just deny myself in food. I deny myself in things I want and things I want to do, and I go without. I've noticed that I've done that most of my life – especially since I died. I cannot let my flesh stand in the way of my walk with God.

I feel Him. He lives with me. He's my companion. And I don't want anything to ever upset that.

Every three months, I take the students of my Bible school on a 3-day fasting retreat. Once they've done it, they want to do it every month!

It changes you. You cannot have the fire of God hit you three or four times a day, and pray, and hear from prophecy, without being changed.

God's Word tells us that when you push back from the table, He comes near you. By us pushing back from the table, confessing our sins and humbling ourselves before God, He comes into the room, and by the second day people are so open to what God has for them.

They have so much pleasure. They get all kinds of breakthroughs at these fasting retreats. They tell me that every time they are healed of something, whether physical, emotional, or financial. And when we are healed, we often get a deeper revelation and understanding of the Word of God.

And that helps us to go out and have a deeper impact on the world around us.

Prayer and fasting will move mountains in your life. I invite you to join me. You can become a mountain mover, too. And when you do, be sure to give God all the praise, glory, and honor! Amen.

Wall of Honor

These are the great men and women of God who inspired me to live for and trust in God. I have been blessed to personally know and reap wisdom from so many great ministry leaders. I am grateful for the many years that God allowed me to spend in the presence of these incredible people.

My Mama, Irene Suddreth (March 5, 1908 – November 21, 1978)

Pastor Lawrence Carswell (Helped him found Church of God churches in the 1960s and early '70s)

A.A. Allen (1950s tent meetings in North Carolina)

Rev. Oral Roberts (1960s tent meeting, North Carolina)

Rev. Richard Hall (1960s, North Carolina)

Rev. Pat Robertson (1975) Miami, my story was featured on 700 Club

TBN (1978 – 2018) I have been blessed to preach 100s of times on the Trinity Broadcast Network in California, Arizona, Miami, Dallas and Atlanta

Dr. Morris Cerullo (1980 – 2019) My spiritual daddy

Rev. John Osteen (1984) John Osteen ordained me and was my overseer

Dr. Cho (1984- 2012)

Dr Ja-Shil Choi (1984 – 1989) My spiritual mama

Dr. Lester Sumrall (1984- 1990) Lester invited me onto his TV show for months at a time and booked me in his churches across the USA.

Pastor Cliff and Kathy Ornduff (1985) Close friends to me and parents to Laurie Crouch– I preached in their church several times

Dr. Andrew Bills (1975 - present) My spiritual son. Founder of the Holy Spirit Broadcasting Network. I frequently appear on his network.

Dr. Lee Benton (1974 - present) My spiritual daughter. I have preached with her many times over the years at CBS studios.

Reinhard Bonnke (2015 – 2019) He was my spiritual covering.

About the Author

Betty Green has committed her life to serving the Lord and spreading the good news of the gospel. She is a graduate of the Morris Cerullo School of World Evangelism. Ordained by John Osteen in 1984, she is still sharing Jesus with everyone who crosses her path.

Over the past 45 years, Betty has started 100+ Bible schools across the United States. She founded 25 churches throughout America and the Caribbean, as well as helping to establish Prayer Mountain in California with Dr. Ja-Shil Choi. During her lifetime in ministry, she has ordained over 3,000 ministers and has written 30+ books.

Betty has been featured on many television programs to share her encounter with hell and her story of redemption. These include: 700 Club, TBN, Maury Povich Show, and the Joan Rivers Show, to name a few. Her story has been told on many more shows across the landscape of Christian television, where Betty has given hope and inspiration to millions.

She enjoys her semi-retirement in sunny Florida, where she still teaches the Word of God to students in her Bible School at Suncoast Cathedral, where she serves under her nephew, Senior Pastor Tim Suddreth.

She also conducts quarterly fasting retreats, as well, and continues to travel and speak all over America.

If you would like to participate in one of her fasting retreats, or if you would like to book Betty to speak at your church or other event, please visit http://www.bettygreenministries.com for contact information.

To see photos, and get free information on prayer, fasting, and other things mentioned in this book, visit http://www.mountainmovingmama.com

Other Books by Reverend Betty Green

From Vice to Victory
Intercession Prayer Manual
The Violent Take it By Force
Can Women Preach?
Angels

Bible School Manuals
The Life of Christ
My Body – His Life
How to Search the Scriptures
Getting Rid of Self
Prayer, Intercession, Travail, Worship
What God Has to Say About Money
Warfare Manual: A Study of All Spirits
Anointing
The Book of Esther
The Book of Ruth
The Authority Christ Gave the Church
Right & Wrong Thinking
Praying God's Word
The Holy Spirit

You can order these books on Betty's website at
www.bettygreenministries.com

Made in the USA
Columbia, SC
17 March 2021